The
Magical Crone

The
Magical Crone

CELEBRATING THE WISDOM OF LATER LIFE

Jennifer Reif
and Marline Haleff

CITADEL PRESS
Kensington Publishing Corp.
www.kensingtonbooks.com

CITADEL PRESS books are published by

Kensington Publishing Corp.
850 Third Avenue
New York, NY 10022

All Kensington titles, imprints, and distributed lines are available at special
quantity discounts for bulk purchases for sales promotions, premiums, fundraising, educational, or institutional use. Special book excerpts or customized
printings can also be created to fit specific needs. For details, write or phone the
office of the Kensington special sales manager: Kensington Publishing Corp.,
850 Third Avenue, New York, NY 10022, attn: Special Sales Department;
phone 1-800-221-2647.

First Printing: September 2003

10 9 8 7 6 5 4 3 2 1

Printed in the United States of America

Designed by Leonard Telesca

LIbrary of Congress Control Number: 2003101243

ISBN 0-8065-2501-0

Contents

Preface

In mid-2001 we began to work on a women's class that we called "The Crone Zone." Two decades of Goddess religion had taught both of us about the Maiden, Mother, and Crone, about this triune cyclic and yet eternal aspect of the Goddess. Here we were, living the latter part of the divine cycle, wanting to personalize our sense of awareness with the Goddess as the Great Crone. One of us having achieved Cronedom and the other well on the way and in the midst of menopause, we felt it was high time to look at the elder woman's life through Pagan eyes.

The very word *crone* needed redefining, needed a new twist. Crones can be not only wise but beautiful and powerful. At the same time, there are many issues that elder women in our culture need to deal with. As we combat negative stereotypes, we look not simply at the value of elder women but at the special magical qualities that are the Divine Crone within.

As we structured the class, we considered the need to bring forward our awareness of the wisdom we have gained in life, of the strength that we have had to develop, and of our deep personal connection to the Goddess. There must be, we thought, a way to share all of this in a magical circle of elder women, in a community of Crones.

This book provides ways to increase our awareness of the Crone within, as well as appreciate our own wisdoms and strengths.

While most of this work can be done as a solitary, the Crone Zone ritual at the end of the book is transforming, and will give you a communal experience with other Divine Crones. All those who are in tune with this book become a part of that community of Crones.

Much that was not only magical and powerful but tender and sweet was brought forward during both the class and its ritual. It is our hope that you gather your elder women friends together, work with the material in the book, and experience the Crone Zone ritual. With love and with blessings for a beautiful and magical life, we bring you *The Magical Crone: Celebrating the Wisdom of Later Life*. Enjoy.

The
Magical Crone

The Crone

—M.H.

What Is a Crone?

As we enter the realm of Cronehood, we reach the third part of our lives. The Crone has many aspects and contains the other two parts of the Triple Goddess—Maid and Mother—within her. Being an elder, she has experienced each stage of existence. She is a matriarch, and as such, is a wise woman and teacher. She can be a leader, a healer, and a source of spiritual and magical knowledge. Within her she has retained her vision of the past and uses this wisdom to plan for the future. Since the Crone is usually at the time of life when she no longer bears children, she has the ability to gather her force once spent in this area and focus her energies and creativity on other matters.

In current Wiccan and Pagan culture, great respect and many positive qualities are attributed to Crones. Because the Crone has lived through life's challenges, she has many stories that teach, entertain, and carry the whole range of human emotions. She is not only a storyteller; she is a priestess, teacher, lover, mother, daughter, sister, and more. She has delved into her spiritual wisdom and knows about the Goddess, the divine seasons of life, and the power of magic and ritual.

As we enter Cronehood, we reassess our values. Crones form a large and important group in our communities. Joining a Crone

Group and writing down our ideas together can be helpful as we investigate what others feel and do. Being a Crone has a physical and a mental/spiritual aspect, so the time when one achieves Cronehood can depend on the individual. In one Crone group meeting, women talked about how they understood their role as Crone. Did entering the Crone phase depend on age, stage of life, feelings about one's role—perhaps a mix of all these? Some thought fifty was the time for Cronehood, while others who were astrologically inclined suggested the Second Saturn Return at age 56. At another Crone meeting there was a woman in her late twenties who felt she had already begun her Crone phase. Typically, Cronehood begins around menopause—around the mid-fifties—although there are varying opinions about its onset, and Cronehood will likely be different for every woman.

The average life span is longer than it was a century ago. The United States Census Bureau posted a high of 77 years for life expectancy in 1999, with males reaching 74.1 years and females 79.7 years for all races. Projections to 2010 give 78.5 as the life expectancy, with 75.6 for males and 81.4 for females.

So, as a larger segment of the population becomes older, moving from middle to old age can mean a significant change in roles. As we tend to be a youth-oriented society, youth is highly valued and older women often fade into the background. However, to be a Crone today means challenging these ideas, for it is at this time in life that women can reach the height of their creative powers. Various scientific data supports this. In *New Passages* by Gail Sheehy, Dr. Frederick Goodwin, director of the National Institute of Mental Health, is quoted as saying that "Psychic prowess actually builds in women as they age." Not to mention that people have been choosing new and fruitful careers at the ages of fifty, sixty and sometimes seventy or eighty.

Cronehood is an increasingly important time in women's lives. A survey of mental attitudes called *The Midtown Manhattan Study* concluded that mental health and well-being improved from generation to generation between the first part of the study in 1954 and the follow-up in 1974. The 1974 data indicated that the happiest people were women aged 40 to 59. Statistics for men indicated, however, age 50 to 59 was the time they were most likely to register as unhappy. According to these statistics, the happiest time in a woman's life is when she reaches and begins to experience her Cronehood.

There may be fear in acknowledging Cronehood, and it can be difficult to find powerful and positive Crone images. Aging men are frequently considered pillars of society, but seldom is the older woman lauded for her gray hairs. Negative stereotypes of the Crone are often encountered, and women approaching Cronehood often complain that they begin to feel invisible, no longer players on the social scene. Some reported internalized images of themselves as being shapeless, sexless, tired, or superfluous. Perimenopause can also bring unresolved problems and bouts of despondence. Looking back on one's past achievements and heading into new phases of mastery and ability in the fifties can help to dispel such downturns. Women in this age range are increasingly moving into the public arena, helping to improve society and better their own way of life.

The devaluing of the older woman is not universal, however, and in cultures that thrived long before our own, her value was often high. Thought of as a wise woman, the Crone was often associated with ritual, magic and healing, especially with the use of herbs. When the belief in the Goddess was strong and women important as priestesses and leaders, the Crone was a revered member of the community.

As the patriarchal Indo-Europeans invaded Asia, Europe, and the Mediterranean areas, however, they brought with them their worship of male gods and hierarchical systems relating to the sexes. The idea of an all-powerful male god and what it implied about the nature of society in such religions as those of the Hebrews, Muslims, and Christians effectively changed the cultures of the worshipers. The result was the systematic devaluing of once-important women: The benevolent herbal healer was changed to an evil witch, intent on "black magic" and other misdeeds. Archaeologist Marija Gimbutas says of the Crone Goddess in her study of Old Europe, *The Language of the Goddess:* "Although degraded to a witch and pushed deep into the forest during the Christian era, she still maintains supernatural characteristics of an important and powerful deity. She is clearly associated with the birds and the Bird Goddess; she flies like a bird or rides on a broom or log . . . she knows the magic of herbs with the help of which she can regenerate life, restore the dead to life and heal sick people and animals."

In the middle ages Crone herbalists and seers were among the first doctors. However, many of these women, denounced as witches, were burned at the stake. Why? Medicine was designated as the province of male doctors, and the healing women, who had from ancient times dispensed herbs, were considered dangerous.

Today Crones accomplish much and lead fruitful lives, although there have always been women who achieved a great deal in their older years, from artists to the public spirited to grandmothers who have played an important part in their family's welfare. You can read about some of these in the next chapter. You might find out something that will move you to venture forth in an imaginative new way.

The season of the Crone is becoming more interesting and pleasurable as her horizons widen. A woman with fewer dependents and more time may now spend her energy on creative work, concentrate on causes that are important to her, or even implement her own business, based on abilities that she has acquired over the years. She may go back to school to continue an education interrupted by marriage, family, or other necessities.

As Crones we can decide what kind of life we want to live and really accomplish our goals. Meditate and write down your perceptions. Many valuable ideas may come from such musings. For example:

- When I think of the definitions of Cronehood, I know that I would like to be a creative and sexy Crone with the understanding to know the world deeply.
- The Crone has done much and can pass on her wisdom where it is needed or give a hand to those who falter.
- As a Crone, I can be a revolutionary. Why fool around? We don't have that much time.
- The Crone has few illusions. She wants to see results.

Linking up with the Goddess as an image of the divine with rituals and magical pursuits can increase your confidence and abilities to truly transform you into the Magical Crone. The Crone has come to know the divine pulse of the Goddess in nature, in every drop of flowing water, and in every leaf that moves in the wind. She can work a magical rite, not only as a tool of transformation, but as a sacred art. In these things the Crone finds great pleasure. The world hums all around her. Behind the whirlwind and stresses of her everyday life is the silent symphony of the spiritual world. The Crone listens, and hears.

Crones are carriers of their culture. The Goddess calls us, and we know the power of the Goddess. It is the Crones who know this, and this knowledge can heal the earth—bring us back into harmony—make the ancient ways new again. For this gift of power and independence, give thanks.

The Crone in Archaeology and History

The importance of the older woman is directly connected to the historical importance of women in relation to their cultures. As far back as the Neolithic (Stone) Age, women had great independence and powers. However, as time progressed, male supremacy became fundamental. The focus changed to worshipping a male god and cultures became focused on military might and the organization of fighting men. Women lost most of their power and authority unless they related to men. The cultures of Old Europe, Asia, and the Middle East were incorporated into this new patriarchal system.

Groups which still retained their goddess orientation through the Bronze Age and into historical times included the Minoans of Crete, the Greeks, the Etruscans in Italy, the Celtic peoples, the Germanic people, and the Balts.

In most nonpatriarchal religions, the third part of life is a time when Goddesses (and women) are concerned with such things as healing, herb craft, the dispensing of justice, magic, divination, the care of the dying, death, and regeneration.

In the Greek pantheon, the Crone Goddess Hecate is descended from the old European goddess of life, death, and regeneration. Athena, born directly from the head of Zeus, was the Hunting Goddess as well as a giver and teacher of crafts—especially weaving and metalwork. Demeter, mother of Persephone, was Goddess of Grain.

As the Maiden is concerned with growth, and the Mother with creation, the Crone in myth rules over death and resurrection. The belief in resurrection is tied in to the idea that life is part of a cycle, and that all things are in some ways recycled. Her knowledge of these things makes her a guide to understanding, spirituality, and change. As a teacher and initiator, she is an agent of personal growth and therefore an important part of life and maturity. She sees clearly the past, present, and future, and her wisdom can be an enhancement of life. Crone Goddesses are found throughout the world, as we will show more fully in other chapters. All these Goddesses are connected to beliefs about the important role of the Crone, but as women became less and less important in their cultures, so did the older woman. The growth of patriarchal attitudes in which women became defined primarily as consorts of men can be seen in changes at various times.

Take the religion of the Hebrews for instance. At one time Hokmah was a representation of maternal wisdom and was mentioned in Proverbs 8 as co-creator with God; in later writings she is rejected and vilified as a concept. In fact, the Hebraic writings have many proscriptions against women and the importance of Goddesses, beginning with Genesis. Eve is created out of Adam's rib and then, at the suggestion of a serpent, eats the apple of the tree of knowledge, source of the understanding of good and evil. Adam follows her lead and they are both thrown out of paradise. The symbols of the Tree of Life and Knowledge, as well as the serpent, icon of the Goddess's powers and connection with the earth, all point to the fact that a new belief system was taking over, inverting the sacred symbols of the old. Many portions of the Bible are devoted to criticism of Israelites and others who continued in the ways of the former Goddess-based religion. Look at the Hebrew daily prayer for men, which states, "Blessed Art Thou O

Lord our God, King of the Universe, who has not made me a woman."

The early Christians had a number of sects that were branded as heretical. These groups were eliminated in favor of the Roman Catholic Church's edicts following the teachings of Paul and Augustine. Along the way, Clement I converted to Christianity, and while busy eradicating other religious beliefs, removed some of the last remaining repositories of ancient knowledge by burning the irreplaceable great library of Alexandria.

Following in the path of the Roman Empire, the Roman Christians began to actualize control by eliminating religious groups not congruent with their interpretations. They instituted a series of inquisitions, beginning with the Albigensian Crusade, which slaughtered the Cathars of Provence and then wiped out a large proportion of Bogomils, Knights Templar, Jews, Waldenses, Fraticelli, and others. These inroads on other sects not only enlarged the territories of the central church but gave the church ownership of all property held by "heretics."

And then the persecution of women began en masse. In 1484, after most of the heretical groups had effectively been eliminated, Pope Innocent VIII issued a Papal Bull against a new kind of heresy: witchcraft. Church laws had taken away women's traditional roles including priestess, healer, midwife, landowner, lawmaker, judge, historian, craftswoman, and teacher. They now were further proscribed by the *Malleus Maleficarum*, "The Hammer of Witches," a book that stated that human females were, by nature, agents and tools of the Devil (a deity previously foreign to religious thinking) and gave instructions for recognizing "signs" of devil possession. These signs ranged from skin blemishes to indications of uniqueness and authority. What followed were three centuries of torture, homicide, and witch burnings in which masses of people were burned alive, 80 to 90 percent of them women. This persecution is likened to the extermination of the Jews by the Nazis during World War II.

The Protestants of the Reformation, though less deadly, did little to change attitudes toward the status of women. Martin Luther said in the *Vindication of Married Life* that the man is higher than

the woman and so must maintain power "for the regiment and do-
minion belong to the man as head and master of the house."
Women were useful in their role as mother, but as she entered her
Crone years, she had no further usefulness despite her knowledge
or abilities.

In the eighteenth and nineteenth centuries, things began to
change. Women began to speak about their oppression and their
inequality in society. In 1792, Mary Wollstonecraft wrote *A
Vindication of the Rights of Woman,* saying of the biblical story of
Eve: "The rights of humanity have been thus confined to the male
line from Adam downwards." The Women's Suffrage movement
brought in more courageous followers and earned women the
right to vote. Throughout the years, women's place in society has
improved. But only in the most recent years have attitudes about
women in their Crone phase begun to change.

Attitudes toward Crone-aged women still include the idea that
these older women have "passed their prime." Since many women
feel their creativity is on the rise at this time in their lives, it is not
surprising that some modern women have made headway in
changing this perception. Woman artists, who are often at the
forefront of thought, have created a large body of work examining
the situation.

One example is Mary Kelly, who has had several exhibitions
dealing with the phases of a woman's life. After confronting motherhood in "Post-Partum Document," she went on to "Interim,"
which explores the crisis of identity experienced by older, post-
maternal women. Kelly's art employs graphic creations to question
the identity of older women. The work is divided into sections. In
"Corpus," fiction, fashion, and medicine are examined; in "Pe-
cunia," family relationships and roles such as mother, daughter,
sister, and wife; in "Historia," the media; in "Potestas," social sci-
ences and the jargon of measurement. Using plastic forms, col-
lage, and various unusual materials, Kelly cuts to the heart of ideas
and feelings relating to the life of older women, illuminating our
understanding of subtle and not so subtle relationships.

The truth is that in these times of increased longevity and
health, many woman and men work long past what we think of as
retirement age. Many start new careers or "get a new lease on life"

in their mid-fifties. Thus the third part of life can be one of great importance and often provides the freedom to do as we wish. At this time in our lives, we may have fewer obligations and a better ability to develop authentic phases of our personalities. It is a time when we can concentrate on who we are and what we really want to do. Nothing can hold us back.

2

Wise Blood

—J.R.

When our monthly bleeding first began, it was our natural rite of initiation into womanhood. Our blood connected us to the Goddess as the Great Birth Mother. We may not have been aware of this sacred connection until Goddess religion became popular. However, even without the spiritual context, menses marks an astounding revelation. It means a female is no longer a child but a woman able to bring new life out of her own body.

Contemporary young Pagan women learn of the Goddess as the Great Creatress who gives birth to all life on earth and see woman as the Goddess's counterpart. As Pagan women our identity with the Goddess grows. As the years pass, we develop a more complex awareness of our relationship with the feminine source of life.

The monthly shedding of blood deeply ties into the Creatress. Mythic images of Goddess-fertility often include the color red: the red apple, the red rose, and the blood-red seeds of the pomegranate. These scarlet images are profound Goddess motifs. Since menses signifies woman's divine fertility, her menstrual blood is seen as holy, potent, and magical. This precious fluid is retained during pregnancy and nourishes the growing child. It is the magical elixir within the golden chalice.

The experience of being present at the birth of a child is one that demonstrates the magic of the Goddess and holds it firmly in memory. Through blood, pain, and travail, the child emerges. Time stands still as the sacred child enters the world from the holy chalice. All who are in the room feel this power. A great light floods the birthplace. Smiles break out on the faces of all those who are present, because the joy of the Creatress permeates the room. It is an immense and undeniable sign of divine power. The spiritual presence of the Goddess has filled the room; it shines and lifts the heart into bliss. Every woman is Goddess. Woman is the doorway from the realm of spirit into physical life.

In our later years our blood is referred to as "Wise Blood" because those who are menopausal metaphorically retain this magical fluid, this power, within them during their years of elder wisdom. The feminine energies that went toward creating a child are now kept within. In this way the Crone keeps a great source of power inside of her.

A menopausal Crone can now direct her energies toward many creative endeavors. Some feel a desire to withdraw a little, spending time contemplating and creating a deeper union with the Goddess. Crones teach the young about life. They teach younger women about their experiences in Goddess religion. While there are many books available on this subject, Goddess religion is essentially an oral tradition with elder women teaching others about their religious path.

Just as a young woman experiences a rite of transition into fertile adulthood, the Crone has a rite of transition into non-bleeding. But unlike the sudden onset of menses, menopause is a transition that can take several years. Hormones shift and women must cope with the changes (see information on "The Hale and Healthy Crone" in chapter 6). Some women will go through a period of sadness and loss. The monthly ritual of the body is no more, and so they grieve at its ending. Others are pleased at the transition, and feel freed from the pain they experienced during menses. All responses to menopause are right and appropriate. There are no wrong feelings during your transition to menopausal Crone.

During your transition, focus on the powers of the Great Goddess; she remains within you after your monthly bloods cease. As we move forward into Cronehood, we may find that some of our views and attitudes change. We find a sense of self-love, determination, and joy that we have not known before. As we get older, many of us discover that we have a new strength to speak out when we feel that something needs addressing, particularly when something seems wrong or unjust.

While this is our time to act and speak out, it is also a time for love and compassion. Having found inner strength does not mean that we have lost our sensitivity or our ability to be compassionate. Compassion is one of the hallmarks of the Goddess. Through the power of our Wise Blood, we can weave together the qualities of strength, grace, and compassion. To meet this challenge, this chapter ends with an exploration of four Goddesses of Wise Blood power. First, we will take a look at the natural transition of physical mortality, and then at our blessing of spiritual immortality.

Facing Our Physical Mortality

Our body is wonderful with a sublime intelligence of its own. Our senses and our ways of perceiving the world are miraculous. We gather information about the world through our hearing, our sight, our sense of smell, our sense of taste, and our sense of touch. More and more, as we journey into the last phase of physical life, we have a greater appreciation of these gifts.

When child-bearing years are over, we enter a new phase of life. The end of menses is a reminder that we physically exist within the world of time, and that this body is not eternal. The recognition that we need to face our physical mortality is fearful to some, but it can be a blessing to all. It brings a kind of ending into our lives, but it also brings a new beginning as wonderful possibilities lay ahead.

We can care for our body so that it continues to serve us, but we understand that it is simply a vehicle that enables our spirit to be carried around through this world. And yet, our body is a sacred and beautiful thing. Being born, living, and dying are a part of the grace, rhythm, and pattern of this world. From the seed, life emerges and bears fruit. The plant can live long, but in the end it always returns to earth. It always returns to the Goddess.

We can face our own death. We can fully accept that the physical body has a beginning and an end, knowing all the while that our spirit is eternal. The acceptance of this creates a dramatic change in our psyche. It becomes easier to let small problems go. Small arguments do not seem so important. We gain the ability to set boundaries in our relationships. More and more, we trust in the Goddess when we face a challenge. We rise up spiritually and our view of the world becomes colored with compassion. These changes in attitude are a part of the Crone's wisdom and Wise Blood power.

Embracing Our Spiritual Immortality

Your essence is beautiful and immortal. Your spirit and your individuality will continue after your body passes away from this world. It is right to embrace and honor physical life while you are a part of it. The physical world is of divine origin. At the same time, know that this place is only one part of the journey of your soul. There is more to come.

The Crone overcomes the fear of death through her wisdom. She learns to embrace the world of the unseen, to embrace the world of spirit. We do this by spending more time engaged in a greater number of activities that have a purely spiritual focus: prayer, ritual, meditation, contemplation, and being of service to others.

When we immerse ourselves in Goddess worship, we are united with the eternal. We gift ourselves with a glimpse of the immortal world. Worshipping at her altar, meditating upon her image, praying with love in our hearts, we contact the beauty of the divine world of spirit. Spend time with the Goddess. No one can do this for you.

When we give of ourselves and serve others of our own free will, purely because it feels right, then we have risen into the world of spirit. We have touched the immortal world where love brings us in contact with divine joy. Every time you can, try to be loving to yourself and loving to others, despite life's many challenges.

As we focus more and more on the Goddess, we increase our awareness of her divinity in all things. She is everywhere. The wind moves the leaves of the trees, birds glide, flowers open and petals fall, seeds grow from damp soil, animals and human beings live, and she is there. Our spiritual goal becomes that of knowing and feeling her divine presence in all things. From June McDaniel's *The Madness of the Saints* we learn that when we focus inward on a religious goal, we actually become more integrated. McDaniel tells us that when we surrender to divinity we "taste bliss" and experience "delight." It is the act of surrendering to the Goddess's divine presence that brings us the pleasurable awareness of the immortal spirit. Through our Wise Blood we come more deeply in contact with the Immortal Goddess. The following prayer can be used as a morning meditation.

To the Immortal Goddess, I Surrender

Mother of One Thousand Names,
I hear Your voice on the wind
As rustling leaves speak Your many names:
Bare Branch, Ripening Fruit, Unfurling Green.
You are all . . . vast and enchanting.
You are every power that is.

In softness and honey comes Your sweet song.
I listen and hear You murmuring within all things.
O Immortal One,
Who is jeweled and crowned with shimmering gold,
How great is Your beauty.
To You, I surrender.

You go on forever . . . beautiful, immortal and divine.
To You, I surrender.
I fall into Your pool of divine beauty
And know that we are One.
O Mother of One Thousand Names,
To You, I surrender.

Four Goddesses of Wise Blood Power

To help meet the challenge of Cronehood, we will explore four feminine energy archetypes from various ancient cultures: Shakti, Yin, Tara, and Binah. In Hindu theology *Shakti* is described as the boundless female principle of cosmic energy. In Asian wisdom it is called *Yin*, the "White Tiger." Yin is recognized as a powerful energy that nourishes and heals. In Tibetan Buddhism she is *Tara*, the personification of Supreme Wisdom and the Universal Mother of all Buddhas. In Cabalistic teachings she is called *Binah*, the Mother of Life, and the Great Sea from which all things are born.

In this section you will find background information on Laksmi (a form of Shakti), on Kwan Yin, on Tara, and on Isis (a form of Binah), as well as some suggested practices with them. Steep yourself in their energies to deepen your awareness of your Wise Blood powers. Focus on one each week. In a month, you will have experienced them all.

Using the verse and poetry that follows the description of each goddess, create brief candle-lighting rituals for each. You might want to personalize your rituals by doing additional research, and/or writing your own additional verse or poetry. You can add icons, statues, or images of each Goddess to your altar. One way to get an image is to copy a picture from a mythology encyclopedia and then frame it in a standing frame.

As you study and work with each Goddess, imagine that her power, her blood, flows through you. Feel the qualities of these Goddesses inside of you. This is your inherited Wise Blood, a gift from your mother's mother's mother, and so on. Your connection to the Goddess goes back long before recorded history. Think of a time long ago when birth was viewed as a magical act, when the cycles of nature were seen as divine, and when stories of Goddesses were told around communal fires. That ancient cultural heritage was filled with respect for Woman as Goddess. For generations upon generations, this heritage was lost to western culture, but now it has returned. Regardless of race, culture, time, or place, this part of the past belongs to you. Remember, and know, the Goddess flows through your veins.

Lakshmi (Shakti): The Creative Female Principle

In Hinduism there are many spiritual texts and many schools of religious thought, some going back thousands of years. These form
the basis of scores of distinct religions, of which *Shaktism* (Goddess Religion) is one. Recorded evidence of Shaktism goes back as
far as 5500 B.C.E. Shakti was celebrated as the ultimate divinity, as
the Divine Mother of the Universe. She was, and is, the Supreme
Creative Energy, worshipped in feminine form.

In India and Bengal, she is known as pure Goddess power. All
of her forms are considered one and the same Goddess. Some of
her most popular forms are Kali and Durga (fierce forms), and
Parvati and Lakshmi (benign forms). Shakti is also the consort of
many Gods and is considered the source of their power. In some
cases, she has been defined as God's feminine aspect; each God has
its Shakti. The prototypical Shakti was the consort of the God
Shiva, who (with Vishnu, a restorative, creating, and manifesting
God) is one of the two primary Gods in post-Vedic Hinduism.

The holy text, the *Artharva Veda*, was composed from an oral
tradition in India. It is a collection of hundreds of hymns, written
down in an archaic form of Sanskrit. From Franklin Edgerton's
The Beginnings of Indian Philosophy, we learn that there is a hymn
from the Artharva Veda dedicated to the Great Mother titled:
"Viraj.": "The Shining One truly was this universe in the beginning. Of her, gods and men said, she is the one who knows that
upon which we may subsist. Let us invoke her."

One of the forms of Shakti is the Goddess Lakshmi. Lakshmi is
the Goddess-power behind Vishnu. One story tells of Lakshmi's
emergence from the churning seas as a Goddess of Beauty and
Good Fortune. She is often pictured standing upon water. From
her ocean of milk, many wonderful treasures come. She is seen
with gold coins in the palm of one hand and a lotus flower in the
other. Around her are many bowls of fruit, seeds, and grains.

In one story, Lakshmi created Soma, the elixir of immortality.
She gave the God Indra a drink of *"Soma,"* or "Wise Blood," from
her body (other versions have the God Indra stealing it from the
craftsman of the Gods). This elixir gave Indra the power of rebirth and immortality.

In Tantric Hinduism, Shakti or Kundalini is the name used for the driving power of the chakra system in the human body. She is the energy that powers the chakra at the base of the spine. A total of seven chakras rise up through the center portion of the body to the top of the head. This energy is considered to be coiled at the base of the spine, like a snake. Ready to be awakened through spiritual exercises, prayer, mantras, or meditations, she rises and gives transcendent spiritual experience and spiritual freedom. This movement of Shakti, or Kundalini, energy, rises through us and is most probably how we experience the pleasure of our awareness of the Goddess as we pray and meditate.

Praying and meditating upon Shakti will bring you in contact with the Goddess as the Supreme Creative Principle. Through her, we recognize our divinity and the creative powers of our Wise Blood within.

Shakti Prayer

I am immortal and of divine origin.
Through me, does the vine bear fruit
And the holy apple tree brings forth its sweet riches,
For I am Shakti.

All that is beauty and goodness comes through me.
I am purity and strength.
I rise up, fearless and bright
Beyond the face of adversity into new creation,
For I am Shakti.

I am wisdom, light, and power.
My will flourishes.
All that I will, nourishes, heals, and bears fruit.
For I am Shakti.
All honor to the Great Mother.

Shakti Ritual

Create a Shakti altar. Include a candle, a bowl of fruit, and a white flower in a vase with green leaves. Use the Shakti prayer above to place you in accord with her power. Repeat it three times to focus on the affirmations. Do this morning and evening. As holds true for all the ritual work suggested in this chapter, you'll need to plan so you are not rushed. Work with your ritual, come into alignment with Shakti, and be inspired to move through your life with power and grace. Let the awareness of Shakti within you rise up and assist you.

Shakti in Action: Generous Giving
After you have worked with your Shakti ritual for one week, go out into your community to actualize her with others. Find a way to serve in a demonstration of this creative female principle. As Lakshmi, give your resources to others. Consider who might need what is appropriate for you to give, then give freely with an open and loving heart. Feel Lakshmi with you. Feel at one with her riches and generosity.

Kwan Yin: The Source of Feminine Power

In Taoist Chinese tradition, Yin (feminine) is seen as the opposite of Yang (masculine). They are not so much opposing powers as they are complementary powers; both are required for Creation and sustaining Creation. Yang is seen in the elements of wood and fire, with qualities that are light, airy, and skyward. Yin is seen in the elements of water and earth, with qualities that are dark, heavy, and earthward.

There seems to be some mixing of these qualities. The black and white Yin-Yang symbol demonstrates this, with its little dot of black in the white field, and vice versa. For the feminine symbol, rather than a dark image, it is the White Tiger, royal, pure, strong, and sleek, that has become the symbol of Yin. From author Barbara Walker's *The Women's Encyclopedia of Myths and Secrets,* we read that Yin is the Chinese name of the feminine life force, and that it is a cognate of the Hindu word "yoni" (sacred term for the female genitals). In addition, Walker describes Yin as "a liquid emanating from the female Grotto of the White Tiger."

The Goddesses and Gods of Chinese mythology do not exist in one single cohesive pantheon. Chinese oral traditions arrive to us via written tales from the pre-dynastic period. Many traditional myths were recorded by philosopher Chuang-tzu (third century B.C.E.). Other influences were the Buddhist tradition from India. The concepts of Yin and Yang are woven throughout these myths with female-male qualities represented as: earth-sky, moon-sun, water-fire, and dark-light. Yin and Yang deities are seen as managing the universe through balancing their powers.

There is one Goddess who has taken on such adoration, she is almost lifted above the duality of Yin and Yang. She is Kwan Yin (*Quan Yin*). She began her history as a Chinese Goddess, and was later adopted by Buddhism. In the book *Chinese Mythology* by John Ferguson, we learn that the worship of Kuan Yin developed under Chinese influence. Though she is now a part of Indian Buddhism, her origin is Chinese. Kwan Yin crossed over into Indian Buddhism as the consort and the source of feminine power for the male deity *Bodhisattva Avalokitesvara* (just as Shakti is the female power behind the Hindu Gods).

Kwan Yin is a beloved Goddess of Mercy and Compassion. She is the Great Mother of China. One of her names is *Sungtzu niang-niang*, Lady Who Brings Children. Sometimes her statue shows her holding a small child. Other times she is pictured holding a sheaf of rice, or a bowl of rice, symbolizing her powers of abundance. She pours water (a primary Yin symbol) from a vase, demonstrating that she governs the Waters of Life, which are not only life-giving but healing and rejuvenating. She is often clad in a white dress, and like other Goddesses, holds a lotus flower. Sometimes she is pictured as having many arms, or standing upon the Red Dragon, which is the male Yang symbol of spirituality, wisdom, and strength.

Kwan Yin is sometimes seated on a lotus. To her left may appear *Shan-ts'ai Tung-tsi* (The Young Man of Excellent Capacities), and to her right, *Lung-Wang Nu* (Daughter of the Dragon-King). A bird bringing her a necklace (beauty) and a willow branch in a vase (Yin symbol) may also accompany her.

Titles for Kwan Yin include Goddess of Fecundity, Protector of Women, Bringer of Rain, The Melodious Voice, Goddess of Mercy and Knowledge, Goddess of Fertility, and The Savioress. She is believed to be the answer for all things.

Kwan Yin is approachable, soft, and loving. She is called Mercy;

she does not judge but forgives and loves. She sustains and heals. All who are in need of comfort may call upon her. From experiencing her compassion, we become more forgiving and can release the pains that others may have brought into our life experience.

Kwan Yin Prayer

Kwan Yin, Lady of Mercy and Compassion,
Many have been my pains and travails.
With Your Waters of Life,
Come and wash these pains away from my soul.
Through You shall I become purified and free.

Holy One,
You are beautiful, and full of grace.
Pearls adorn My Lady of Compassion.
And your soft robes are white and glistening.
You smile and the pain of the past falls away
Like dry leaves in Autumn.

Peace and tenderness are with you.
Your simple presence brings healing to body and soul.
Come, Beloved Mother,
Raise my soul high beyond the pains of mortal cares.

Bless me with deep compassion.
So that I may bless others in Your name.
All praise and honor to Kwan Yin.

Kwan Yin Ritual

On your Kwan Yin altar include a candle, a bowl of uncooked rice, a cup or small vase of water, and pearls or a beautiful necklace. Have pen and paper ready. Light your candle. Read the Kwan Yin prayer every evening for one week. During that week, compile a list of what needs forgiving in your life. There may be someone in your life that you need to forgive or perhaps you need to forgive yourself for something you did.

This is an opportunity to confront something in your life that is unresolved. Look at your list. In your compassion, try to find a way to understand what happened. Understanding a negative event does not mean that it will somehow happen again, it simply means that you are able to objectively observe how and why it happened. On the seventh evening, include an act of forgiving in your ritual. Place your truest feelings into your ritual as you read from your paper. Burn the paper. Forgive and then let it all go. You will remember the past, and honor all that happened, but you can still release these things with compassion. To do this is to become Kwan Yin. She is an important part of your Wise Blood.

Kwan Yin in Action: Compassionate Healing

After the week of your Kwan Yin ritual, decide how you can demonstrate her aspect of healer. What can you heal? Perhaps a relationship. Is there some communication with another person that you need to have? Do you want to heal something in your relationship? Summon up your courage and go ahead, but make sure your communication will not be a destructive force. Truth does not mend all relationships. It will, however, mend you. If you cannot communicate, then write it all out.

Perhaps it is your own body that needs healing. Is there something you can do to make yourself healthier? (See "The Hale and Healthy Crone" in chapter 6.) Putting an end to an unhealthy habit or adding a healthy one might be an act of healing for you. Volunteer at a local hospital or donate time or money or blood to the Red Cross. Consider what you might add to your community in the capacity of healing. Go out into the world and become Kwan Yin, the Healer.

Tara: The Supreme Goddess

Among the people of Tibet, China, and India, Tara is the Great Goddess of Buddhism. Her titles include Goddess of Supreme Wisdom, Universal Mother, She Who Delivers, and Great Star. She is known as a Goddess of Compassion, of Wisdom, and of the Arts. With twenty-one forms, she is a most beloved and revered Goddess, the White Tara and the Green Tara being her most popular forms. Green Tara is called *Bribsun* in India and *Dal Jyang* in Tibet. White Tara is known as *Shveta Tara* in India and *Wen-Chen* in China.

As a Goddess of both the Sea and the Stars, she is invoked for safe journeys across the ocean. Her forms are as varied as the sea itself. Green Tara and White Tara are her benign forms—calm and placid. Blue, Red, and Yellow Tara are her stormy and fierce forms. She is known as a leader of sea nymphs who rescue sailors in danger. As a Sea Goddess, Tara aids in difficult journeys of any kind. She destroys fears, removes obstacles, and bestows boons.

Tara is sometimes pictured sitting cross-legged on a lotus-throne (like Kwan Yin) floating on the sea. A red sash crosses her bare breasts. Eyes of wisdom are on her palms and forehead. A many-petaled golden flower is held in her raised left hand, while her right hand leads the eye downward to her lotus throne. On her head rests an elaborate golden headdress encrusted with gems.

Tara Prayer

Lady Tara, Queen of the Stars,
You cast Your silver light upon the seas.
Crowned and seated upon Your lotus throne
You reign over all, shining and beautiful.

Mother of Knowledge and Compassion,
Light streams unending from Your divine eyes.
With loving you gaze into the hearts of all.
You see and know all things, yet you are gentle.

Great Creatress, from You all royal arts are born;
With Your wisdom, You hold the knowledge of every noble
  craft.
O Tara of the Golden Crown, with rubies red and pearls
  shining,
Goddess, most beautiful and wise, to You I bow.

Tara Ritual

On your Tara altar include a yellow or golden flower, a candle, several silver stars scattered across the altar (you can cut these out of paper and paint them), and red gemstones or red beads. Repeat the above verse one time. Bow to Tara at the end of the recitation. Envision her. Pause and let Tara come to you. The act of bowing, or paying homage, allows her to enter your being. Coming into union with her stimulates creativity and brings enormous joy to the soul. Meditate upon Tara and become aware of this powerful form of the Goddess that lies within you.

Tara in Action: Joyful Creativity
As a Goddess of wisdom and of the arts, Tara can inspire your creativity. Choose one of the craft items in chapter 7 or make something that you have been thinking about making. Choose something that excites and interests you so that you will experience joy in its creation.

Perhaps you have wanted to take an art class or make a quilt or carve wood or simply draw pictures with crayons. Find that art class, procure the tools you need, buy a large box of crayons. Produce something beautiful and wonderful. Consider that as you work, that Tara, the Goddess of All Arts, is with you. Work her magic. Her powers of creativity flow through you.

Binah (Isis): Mother of Earth, Sea, and Heaven

Binah is the name of a Hebrew letter. Its meanings are explained in a text of mystical Judaism called the Kabbala. The Kabbala presents a pattern, or order, of the emanations of the various forces of the universe. These successive emanations form the Tree of Life. Each emanation relates to a Hebrew letter. Binah is the "Third Emanation," that is, the third force of creation on the Kabbalistic Tree of Life. The emanations are said to originate from the "Limitless Light" known as *Ain Soph Aur*.

The emanation of Binah is the Mother, while her partner *Chokma* is the Father (Chokma is wisdom, idea, and will). Binah is considered the cosmic energy that is the source of all creation, of all form. She is the Great Creatress. Binah not only creates; she transforms what remains at life's end and turns it into new life. The Hebrew letter of Binah contains three wave-like glyphs that are emblematic of the sea; from the sea come all primordial things.

The mystical pantheon of the Hermetic Order of the Golden Dawn (origin in the early twentieth century, later made popular by authors Dione Fortune and Israel Regardie) sees the Egyptian Goddess Isis as the primary corresponding Goddess for the emanation of Binah. Isis is the Supreme Mother of Earth, Sea, and Heaven. She is the Divine Mother of Egypt, whose universal appeal sees her as creating, protecting, and nourishing all things. Isis and Binah are two names for the same Wise Blood power.

The name Isis evokes beauty and mystery. The beauty of carnelian and lapis lazuli around her neck, dark hair crowned with the golden Uraeus serpent, the scent of sweet libanum and blue lotus flowers on her altar—these are one with her name. Sometimes she is pictured standing, holding the ankh (a sign of life). Other times she is seated with her glorious wings outstretched, ready to embrace and protect us all.

Much like the ritual mysteries of the Greek Goddess Demeter, Isis also sorrowed and wandered until her myth was resolved. The Mysteries of Isis were focused on death, resurrection, and rebirth. Isis has the power to bear life and regenerate the dead. Just like the Cabalistic Binah, Isis transforms death into life. Her resurrection of the God Osiris is emblematic of this power.

In one of her forms, Isis is equated with Egypt itself. She awaits the fertile overflow of the Nile (seen as the power of her husband Osiris). Blocking this attempt at creation is the God Seth (the brother and rival of Osiris), who is equated with drought. He blocks the union between Isis and Osiris by killing Osiris and dismembering him, scattering his remains across the world.

Isis wanders, sorrowing, in search of the pieces of the body of Osiris. She finds them and reassembles them. She replaces the missing phallus with one of gold (some versions say clay). With magical song, embalming, incantation, and through the beating of her great wings over his body, Isis brings Osiris back to life. Osiris is reborn as Horus. When the Nile is free to overflow, the grain emerges, a symbol of the resurrection of Osiris. Through this myth, Isis is shown as a Goddess of great magical powers.

Through Isis, there is love between woman and man and marriage is sanctified. Through her power, children are born. The right are made strong, the unjust are punished, and the oath is made sacred. Isis protects and grants mercy, yet she is also a Queen of War when war is needed. She is the Mother of Nature and the Queen of the Elements. She is the Queen of Seamanship, and creates good navigation for sailors. Through Isis all things are possible; she is a Goddess who can overcome Fate. We approach Isis in supplication. Through her we find love and the answer to all things. Through her powers we can banish obstacles and work magic to create change and rebirth in our lives.

Isis Prayer

I call Isis, the One whose power created the stars and the
   sun,
Whose power created the great earth, and rivers that flow
   to the sea.
Hail Isis, who made all creatures live and breathe,
Who feeds us and cares for us.
Isis, it is to You I pray.

Lady, all that lives, and dies and is born again,
Does so under Your command.
Great One who derives life from death,
I call upon You to rebuild a part of my life.

Beautiful Goddess, Crowned with the golden Uraeus,
In gold, lapis, and carnelian, Your adornments shine.
Your dark eyes hold the power of the ages,
And Your great wings are ready to awaken
What has been in shadow.

You begin to chant, your sound so ancient,
That you move me beyond time and memory.
With words of power, You hover above me,
Beating Your wings, You begin my transformation.

I feel the rhythm of Your wings.
I hear You speaking across my soul:
"I am Isis, through Me shall you be reborn,
I command the powers of the world,
To aid and support you in your desire.

"Give to me all that is unsure and unknown,
And I will re-create it and make it known.
Give to me that which has died, and I will make it live
  again.
Through Me You will be reborn.
I beat my wings above you; I chant and speak words of
  power

"And so your dreams unfold and flower within you.
It will be so. My power is great, for I am Isis."
Yes, your dreams flower within you.
And dreams becomes reality, by the power of Isis.

Isis Ritual

Set your altar with a candle, frankincense, tumbled carnelian stones (can be found at a gem or mineral store), and a drawing of golden wings outstretched. Have pen and paper at hand. Write down something that you wish to change about your life. Choose something that has been a stumbling block, something that you have failed at, something you feel you want to conquer. Light the candle and read the Isis prayer. Ask Isis for assistance. Do this every night for seven nights. During the day, imagine Isis above you, her great wings protecting you, sending you her power. When you go to bed, imagine that she embraces you with her wings.

Hold fast to your dream and allow Isis to change your life. Have faith and patience. Keep Isis in your heart and she will create this transformation for you. When your transformation is complete, honor her with flower petals cast onto water, tossed into the air from a high place. As you cast the flower petals in homage, say: "Hail Isis!"

Isis in Action: Nurturing Others

Isis is the Great Mother of life, nurturing and caring for her children. For an action emblematic of this, choose a way to nurture others in your community. Some animal shelters need help to pet cats or walk dogs. These animals can benefit from your love. If you have a local women's shelter, call and ask how you can be of assistance. Some hospitals have programs that allow volunteers to feed and cuddle newborns that are being given up for adoption ("Granny Programs").

Perhaps there is something you can do that is close at hand. Do friends or fellow employees seem stressed out? Offer a shoulder massage. Look around you. Who needs nurturing? As Isis, answer that call.

You are Crone. Your Wise Blood is a potent force. You are Shakti and Isis. You are Tara and Kwan Yin. In your wisdom you can weave together strength and compassion. You can weave together the ability to set boundaries, and to be giving and loving. The art of your Wise Blood moves you through the world with wisdom and grace. The ancient Goddess sparkles anew, alive in your veins, sometimes silent, sometimes outspoken, but always the Immortal Creatress whose hand can reinvent the world.

3

The Crone as the Triple Goddess

—J.R. & M.H.

Triple Goddesses abound in many ancient Pagan religions. Triads seem to have special power: the Greek Three Graces, the Scandinavian Three Fates, the Triune aspects of the Celtic Goddess Brigit, and the Roman Triple Matronae are just a few. Three times three brings us the Nine Muses. The numbers three and nine convey a special magic, as found in the traditional Wiccan spell, "and now by the powers of three times three, as we will it, so shall it be!" In numerology, nine is the number of completion and manifestation, while three—consider the triangle and the pyramid—brings strength and stability of form.

The three Goddess archetypes, Maiden, Mother, and Crone, can be a way to view the life of the Elder Woman. As an elder, you have been the pre-pubescent Maiden, the fertile Mother, and the wise Crone. You contain all three aspects.

Your Maiden aspect brings you a fresh approach, as well as the enjoyment of new discoveries and experiences. The Maiden's heart is alive with the joy of life. She is portrayed in the color white as new beginnings, planting, and new growth, with images of the bee, the bow and arrow, the budding blossom, all spring flowers—especially the lily—and the new or waxing moon.

Your Mother aspect gives you the desire and power to bring things into creation. The satisfaction of creation is the reward of the Mother. She is also a caretaker and instinctively nourishes others. She plants, creates, and tends her garden. She has an inborn desire to see life thrive. The Mother is connected with the color red, noon, completion, mature growth, grain fields, the harvest of fruits, the cornucopia, the chalice, the apple, the rose, the sheaf of grain, and the full moon.

Your Crone aspect brings you the ability to form knowledge out of past experiences and to move through the world with wisdom. Compassion tempers the strength of the Crone. She is in the last phase of life. Through the wisdom of the Triple Goddess, she recognizes that death is the night before the dawn. The Crone integrates this wisdom in her cauldron and is renewed by its magic. She drinks of it and shares it, so that those she leaves behind will benefit from the cauldron's blessings. The Crone is connected with the color black, night, endings, the fallow field, the cauldron, caves, the spider and web, the owl, the raven, and the waning or dark moon.

Origins of the Triple Goddess

There are many images and symbolic correspondences for the Triple Goddess. These images and their totems and symbols come to us via the influences of time, place, and peoples. It is the land itself, the body of woman, the world of the animals, the seasons, and the forces of the elements that have shaped the myths of Maidens, Mothers, and Crones. Societal values also shape myths and some of them come to us as deeply influenced by patriarchy. We cannot ignore this, and occasionally it appears as we read the old myths.

There are those who consider myths as static holy objects. They are not. The Greek myths that were written down by Homer, the Roman myths that were recorded by Ovid, the Celtic myths that come to us from the *Mabinogion,* and more, were all, like the Christian bible, written down by human hand, just as a camera takes a photograph as a view of a particular moment from a certain time and place. While ancient poets have provided snapshot views of myths for us, cultural myths are actually evolutionary in nature. Over time, they become influenced by the effects of societal views and by neighboring or conquering cultures. There is no one pure image of any deity—only many views, from many times and places. The divinity of the earth, the mountains, and the flowering meadows speak to us of the original divinity that created life and its myths. To that source of inspiration we can return. We are valid observers of life. Tales that follow, such as the tale of Blodeuwedd, the Flower Maiden, sometimes contain the patriarchal views of their particular society. Some myths may not seem resonant for the time we live in. We have the right to reshape myths for our time. Therefore, while I give you the tales of Blodeuwedd, and also of Rhiannon, I offer up alternate versions for your perusal.

The Maiden, Mother, and Crone are all around us. In nature, and in our own lives, we see the universal triune: beginning, middle, and end—of birth, life, and death. Every new beginning is like the dawn, akin to a budding blossom. Day brings growth and completion. Night brings ending and rest, but like the moon, it leads us back to the waxing dawn. The Night-Crone is reborn as the Dawn-Maiden. Our day, our year, our lives all contain the circular pattern of Maiden, Mother, and Crone. Aspects of the Triple Goddess have been named in many cross-cultural myths around the world. Below we will explore some of the Celtic, Hindu, Native American, Greek, Roman, and Scandinavian forms.

Maidens

Blodeuwedd *("Flower-face," Welsh)*

According to the post-Christian collection of Welsh tales called the *Mabinogion,* the Welsh Maiden Blodeuwedd was born from the flowers of the oak, the flowers of the broom, and the flowers of meadowsweet. She was said to have nine powers, nine buds of plant and tree. She was created through magic, by Gwydion, to be the wife of the hero-God *Llue* (Lug).

In a twist of infidelity, Blodeuwedd falls in love with Gronw Bebyr, who tries to kill Lleu. Blodeuwedd runs into the hills with her maids. The maidens all walk backwards, to face their pursuers, except for Blodeuwedd. The others fall to their deaths into the lake below the hills, but Blodeuwedd lives. As a punishment for her infidelity, Blodeuwedd is transformed into an owl (Crone totem) by Gwydion, to live and hunt at night. The ancient Welsh word for "owl" is Blodeuwedd.

While the post-Christian era may have turned an ancient naturalistic tale into the patriarchal story of the unfaithful wife, we can reclaim the simple beauty of the image of the Welsh Maiden created from flowers. In an alternate version, it is dawn. A magical mist rises from the flowers of the oak, broom, and meadowsweet. The mist turns and coalesces in sweet fragrance until it finally takes the shape of a beautiful Maiden. Flowers stream from her hair and images of them shift and move in her long flowing garment. She is called Blodeuwedd.

Blodeuwedd takes a lover, Lleu, a great warrior. They are happy together, but another warrior sees Blodeuwedd and falls in love with her. His name is Gronw Bebyr. Her lovers meet and fight. Blodeuwedd escapes the battle. She retreats into the mountains, but does not go alone. Some of her maids choose to follow her. The mountains are green and beautiful and the spirit of the mountain asks Blodeuwedd and the maidens to remain. They fall in love with the peace and beauty that they find. Through the magic of the mountains, by day they appear as Flower-Maidens, and by night they appear as owls.

Sarasvati (*"Flowing One," Hindu*)

Sarasvati began as an ancient river of northwest India that flows from the Himalayan mountains toward the sea. The river disappears underground prior to reaching the sea. Bathing in her waters cleanses all impurities.

Dark-eyed Sarasvati is depicted as a graceful young woman wearing white, seated on a lotus. There is a slender crescent moon on her brow. She has four arms and these hold the symbols of her power. With one hand she holds out a flower to her consort-husband, *Brahma*. With another, she holds a book. In another is a string of sacred beads and in another is a little drum. Other images show her as two-armed, playing a stringed musical instrument like a lute called a *vina*.

Sarasvati began the arts of letters, language, calendars, mathematics, and music. Through her, humans learned to communicate, to write their stories—both sacred and secular—and to make music in emulation of the divine spheres. Sarasvati was the dawn of culture and civilization. In India, she is honored in libraries with offerings of flowers, fruit, and incense.

Turquoise Maiden *(Navajo, Native American)*

Her story begins when a great storm occurs on Giant Spruce Mountain (Gobermador's Knob in northwest New Mexico). From that storm, Turquoise Maiden emerged. She was raised by First Man and First Woman. When Turquoise Maiden had her first menses, the first *Kinaalda,* a four-day ceremony and celebration that transformed the Maiden into Changing Woman began.

First Woman dressed Turquoise Maiden with beads of jet, turquoise, coral, and obsidian. She dressed her in a beautiful woven white dress with white moccasins and white leggings. Corn of every color was brought to the festivities. A white belt with white tassels, like corn tassels, was tied around the Maiden's waist. As First Woman brushed her hair, she brushed into it thought, life, and value. These things equal *hozho,* or beauty, for the Navajo.

Each morning of the four days, the Maiden Goddess ran to the east, toward the sun, toward beauty. Each day, First Woman massaged her, impressing into her body the power and strength of womanhood. After the Kinaalda, the Maiden became Changing Woman and was able to bear children. Later, as Changing Woman, she bore twins who made the world safe for her people.

Artemis *(Greek)*

"Where has Artemis not danced?" is a Greek saying. She was worshiped with ecstatic dancing and was called the Virgin Huntress, Goddess of the crescent moon. The herb artemisia was named for her. (Also known as the medicinal herb mugwort, artemisia was used to encourage delivery in birth.) The herb wormwood, or *Artemisia absinthium,* was also named after her. She was summoned to aid women during childbirth and was known to protect anyone who asked for her aid, particularly women threatened by men.

As Greek Goddess of the wilds, connected to tree cults and the world of animals, Artemis represented fertility and vegetation.

After the Mycenaean Greeks came in contact with Crete, the island's Goddesses, such as Britomartis, Diktynna, Ariadne, and Aphaea, were absorbed in the name of Artemis. The Minoan Goddess Eileithyia was also identified with her. A Goddess of birth, Artemis was worshiped in her cave at Amnisos in Crete. She was also revered in Asia, site of the famous statue Artemis of Ephesis, with its many breasts—symbols of nourishment.

One of the myths of Artemis involves Actaeon, who discovered her bathing in a sacred place. It is said that she did this at her yearly appearance, or *anodos*, when she renewed her virginity in the water and took another lover. Although Actaeon knew it was forbidden, he ventured closer, and she discovered him spying. She turned him into a stag, and her hounds then tore him to pieces. This story is probably related to the custom of designating a Stag King who rules for a set period and then is sacrificed or deposed by a challenger. The image of a man with stag horns goes back to paleolithic cave paintings (20,000 B.C.E.) at Spain's Altamira or Caverne des Trois Frères, in France, where it is believed to be related to hunting or fertility magic.

Hestia *(Greek)*

The virgin goddess of the hearth. A deity of fire, Hestia is seen in the center of every home where she symbolizes family unity and protects the house. The Greeks did not consider a new home established until a woman brought fire from her mother's hearth to light her own. All Greek towns had a public hearth, the *Prytaneum*, where Hestia was worshiped and offered sacrifices of first fruits and young animals. She was called Prytantis and her flame represented the social contract of her people. When colonists established a new place, they brought with them fire from their mother city's public hearth. Hestia's temples were always circular. At Delphi, which was considered the center of the universe, her hearth was especially important because it stood for all of Greece. Hestia was the first child born to Cronus and Rhea, and thus had precedence, so at festivals she was poured the first and last libations. At sacrifices the first morsels of victims were given to her. On Olympus, her dignity was unquestioned. Plato said, "In the dwelling of the gods, Hestia alone maintains repose." As a Goddess of fire, she was not often represented in sculpture, but there is a statue of her at Paros, and Glaucus of Argos created one for Olympia.

Persephone *(Greek)*

The maiden Persephone, or Kore, daughter of the Mother Goddess Demeter, is part of an agricultural myth from Crete that accounts for the seasons with their fertile and infertile periods. Persephone and Demeter care for the grain and growing things. One day Persephone is wandering through the fields picking flowers when she hears the call of the dead, who lie beneath the earth. She goes below to care for them, preparing them for the regeneration of life. While she is away Demeter mourns for her daughter. The weather changes and the crops stop growing. After a few months, Persephone returns through a cleft in the earth. The mother and daughter are full of happiness, for they are no longer separated. However, each year the daughter must return to the land of the dead. The mother awaits her until spring brings the renewal of growing things. In this respect, Persephone is also a death and renewal goddess—an aspect of the Crone.

A later version in the Homeric hymns tells the story differently, centering it on the Olympian Gods. Zeus promises Persephone to his brother Hades, the Lord of the Dead. She goes out to the fields to pick flowers. The earth opens up and she falls into the underground kingdom where Hades keeps her prisoner. Demeter is furious, but Zeus will do nothing, so she withdraws her vital energy from the world, letting crops die and lie fallow. She wanders the earth disguised as an old woman. At Eleusis, she is discovered to be a Goddess and asks that a temple be built for her, teaching the queen, Metaneira, the sacred rites that later become the famous Eleusinian Mysteries. Zeus begs Demeter to resume her sacred work, but she refuses unless her daughter is returned. Persephone comes back amid great rejoicing, but in Hades, she was tricked into eating a pomegranate seed, food of the dead. So each year she must spend some time with the Lord of the Underworld. At that time, Demeter mourns her daughter and nothing on the earth grows.

Diana *(Roman)*

The Roman version of Artemis, who is called many-breasted because she created and nourished all living things. As a Lunar Virgin, she had festivals in her honor May 26 to 31 and August 13 and 15, which related to changes of the seasons. Diana's name is taken from the word for "light," and she may have been the original, pre-Roman sun Goddess. She was also a Goddess of mountains and woods, where her sacred places were found.

Her sanctuary at Lake Nemi, called "Diana's Mirror," was known for the way in which her priest was chosen. In the Wood of Nemi there grew a sacred tree, from which only a runaway slave was allowed to break a branch. It was said that this branch was the Golden Bough taken by Aeneas at the Sibyl's bidding as a talisman before he traveled into the world of the dead. The taking of the branch enabled the slave to compete for the priesthood by killing his rival in single combat. From then on, he had to protect his role from all challengers, until he, too, was slain and supplanted.

Fire was important in the rituals at Nemi, for at her yearly festival on August 13, Diana's grove was lit with many torches brought by her worshipers. Diana herself, carrying a torch in her right hand, was represented in bronze figurines found at her precinct. She was honored with a shrine on the Aventine Hill in Rome, where women would come with offerings and invocations.

Vesta *(Roman)*

The Roman counterpart of Hestia. Originally a Goddess of earth and fire, the Romans worshiped her only as the Goddess of the hearth fire and the fire of ceremonials. She also presided over meals and was offered the first food and drink. The Vestalia was her festival, celebrated on June 7. Her sanctuary was visited by mothers of families who brought plates of food. Otherwise it was only accessible to the Vestal Virgins. The Vestal Virgins had great importance in Rome. Under Numa, there were two. Later, Servius increased them to six. They were chosen from patrician families by lot and served for thirty years, taking a vow of chastity. When they appeared in public, a lictor preceded them, protecting the way. If a condemned man chanced to meet one, he was reprieved immediately. Representations of vestals on coins always show them veiled.

Mothers

Danu *(Dana or Anu in Ireland; Don in Wales)*

Danu was the Great Mother of the insular Celtic mythological world. The entire lineage of the *Tuatha De Danann* (People of the Goddess Dana) is based on their divine heredity to her. In Irish literature the Tuatha De Danann are a race of Gods who represent the powers of the light. They battle the Fomoiri, half-humans, half-monsters who have come from outside Ireland and who represent evil. In Welsh tales the similar "Children of Don" are more human, yet have magical abilities with which to fight off their enemies.

Danu (Anu) has strong associations to the fertility of Ireland. In County Kerry there are two round hills that were considered to be the breasts of the Goddess. They continue to be called the "Paps of Anu." The Celts believed that they lived upon the body of their Mother Goddess, gaining life and sustenance from the land itself. They, like many other ancient peoples, lived and breathed their connection to the natural world.

Rhiannon *("Great Queen," Welsh)*

Here is another Welsh myth that takes a powerful Goddess and dis-empowers her: The Goddess Rhiannon rode a magical horse that no other horse could catch. She had a beautiful singing voice; it was a voice of power. Sometimes she sang and butterflies emerged. She married Pwyll, who was a ruler in the otherworld. They had a son named Pryderi, who succeeded his father as ruler. Unfortunately, Rhiannon was unjustly accused of murdering her son and was punished by being forced to carry visitors to the court on her back, in horse fashion. In the end, she was forced to wear the collar of an ass around her neck. So ends the traditional tale.

A new version of the story of Rhiannon shows her motherly love and her magical powers. In it, the Goddess Rhiannon married the God Pwyll. Together they ruled as King and Queen in a land of the otherworld. Their people were famous for their very fine flying horses. Rhiannon won every sky race with her beautiful gray-winged horse, Pegani. When Pegani flew, Rhiannon was filled with so much joy that she would sing. Her singing created beautiful birds and butterflies. As Pegani flew, there were usually purple and white butterflies trailing after him.

Rhiannon taught her son Pryderi to ride in the sky. As a child he was unsure of his winged steed and one day he fell from a great height. Like the wind, Rhiannon and Pegani flew down and caught young Pryderi before he fell to the ground. Rhiannon returned her son to land safe and sound. At once she placed him on an ancient standing stone. Riding her horse around the stone, she circled it many times and sang a magical charm of safety into her son's soul. Never again would her son fall. When Pyrderi grew to be King, he rode his winged stallion through the skies and was able to visit every province in his lands. He learned to understand and care for the needs of his people and so they gave him the title Pryderi the Wise Who Sees All.

Uma *("Mother Goddess," "light," Hindu)*

Uma is a loving mother, who mediates between the Gods when necessary. She is a peacemaker. She is the light that allows for perception, and therefore knowledge. People have awareness through her power.

Uma feeds the world with life-sustaining fruits and vegetables. These are born from her body during the rains. She is the power of germination, and therefore is also a Grain Goddess. She loves well-tended fields and all manner of orderly creation. Like many Hindu deities, her vehicle is the Sacred Cow.

Okanagon Earth Mother *("The Mother of Everyone," Native American)*

The story of this Native American Earth Mother presents the earth itself as a deity. It says that the "old one" made earth from woman, so that she would be the mother of all. They say that the earth is a being, even though we cannot see her. Her flesh is the earth, her hair is the trees and plants, her bones are the rocks, and her breath is the wind. We live on her body. She shivers when it is cold, she sweats when it is hot, and she moves in earthquakes.

Demeter *(Greek)*

Demeter, the earth mother, is primarily the Goddess of plants and the cultivation of foods. She is a grain Goddess, who is worshiped as the giver of plentiful crops. Demeter was always given offerings in their natural state, untouched by fire. Unpressed grapes, uncooked grain, honeycombs, and unspun wool were placed on her altar. At the city of Eleusis, the Greeks annually celebrated mysteries, which centered about Demeter and the myth of her reunion with her daughter. Those who attended this three-day ritual were called the *mystai*. The events were so secret that no one ever revealed them, although the most important writers and thinkers of Greece were proud of attending. Demeter herself has many aspects and names: Demeter Erynes, (Angry); Demeter Thesmophoros (Lawgiver); and Demeter Louisa (Kindly One).

Rhea *(Greek)*

The Aegean Mother Goddess. A Triple Goddess of Crete, she had several names and functions, such as Dictinna the lawgiver of Mt. Dicte and Aegea, who founded the Aegean civilization. One of her titles was Rhea Kronia, Mother Time. She may be related to Rha, the Red One, of Russia, and Rhiannon, the Celtic Goddess. In Hellenic Greece, she was one of the Titans and had a consort, Cronus, Father Time. Their children were Hestia, Demeter, Hera, Hades, Zeus, and Poseidon.

Hera *(Greek)*

A sky queen who ruled earth and all its creatures. Her name means "Our Lady." Known as a Goddess of women and their sexuality, she was worshiped in the festival of Heraea near Hera's town of Argos. It featured 160-yard races in which women ran barebreasted with their hair unbound. There were three groups of runners—young, mature, and old—and a prize was given to each. The winner had the right to leave a statue of herself on Hera's shrine. Like Athena, Hera also had a yearly ceremony in which her worshipers carried her image to water, bathing and renewing it for another cycle of birth, maturity, and death.

Zeus, who was said to have raped and married his mother,

Rhea, also married his sister Hera. The marriage was not a happy one, and Zeus was known for raping and seducing other women. There were many skirmishes of this sort throughout the Greek territory, probably emblematic of the conquest and takeover of the Goddess-oriented matristic* cultures by the patriarchal.

Juno *(Roman)*

The Roman Great Mother. Every Roman woman was once supposed to have a soul, or "juno," as men had a genius. In later, more patriarchal times, the word was dropped. Before the Roman era, Juno was worshiped among the Umbrians, the Oscans, the Latins, the Sabines, and the Etruscans. Her name may have derived from the Sabine-Etruscan Uni, a three-in-one deity whose name has a relationship with "yoni," the word for female genitalia. The original female Capitoline Triad was Juventas, Juno, and Minerva—Maiden, Mother, and Crone. Juventas was supplanted by the god Jupiter in the trinity, which had a temple on Rome's Capitoline Hill. The goddess had many aspects such as Juno Regina, Queen of Heaven, Juno Februe, Goddess of erotic love, and Juno Populonia, Mother of the People.

As moon Goddess, Juno held the titles of Lucetia and Lucina. Lucetia was the feminine principle of celestial light, while Lucina was the Goddess of childbirth, bringing the newborn baby into the light. In this respect, she was an important part of ceremonies of marriage and family events, from Juno Pronuba, watching over the marriage arrangement, to Juno Sospita, who presided over the time of labor and delivered the baby. Sospita, who was shown armed with spear and shield, had two temples in Rome and one in Lanuvium. Guarded by a serpent, it was the site of a yearly ceremony of omens.

Juno Lucina was a symbol of the Roman matron. Consort of Jupiter, she stood in the temple of the Capitoline Triad as Juno Regina holding a golden scepter and thunderbolt. Her festivals were the Matronalia, which were celebrated at the Kalends of

---

*Matristic is a term used by Marija Gimbutas and others to refer to cultures in which the Creator is believed to be female.

March by Roman matrons. At this time it was the custom for the mistress of the house to receive a present from her husband and serve her slaves at the table.

Juno Moneta, the adviser of those who were to marry, expanded her duties to being adviser of the Roman people. Her sacred animals, the geese, warned the defenders of Rome when the Gauls attempted to scale the walls of the citadel of the Capitol. In Latin, *monere* means "to warn." The name for money was derived when a mint that coined currency was built near the temple of Juno Moneta.

Another aspect of Juno was Goddess of battle, representing the fighting spirit of a mother defending her children. Under the name Caprotina, she was a Goddess of fertility, while as Juno Populonia she watched over the multiplication of the race.

Freya *(Scandinavian)*

The Norse Goddess of fertility and love, Freya was the Great Goddess of the north. She was the leader of the Afliae, the primal matriarchs or divine grandmothers. She was also the Vanadis, ruling ancestress of the Vanir, who were the Gods before the arrival of the patriarchal Aesir.

Freya wears the necklace of the Brisings. She paid dearly for it by spending the night with each of the four dwarves who forged it. After she got it from them, it was stolen from her by Loki to give to Odin. The divisive Loki gave it back to Freya in exchange for the promise that she would stir up war in Midgard and set the kings at each other's throats. In myth, it is the king's function eventually to die for the land and his people, while the Goddess never dies. She weeps over him and gives birth to the divine child who takes his place. Following the pattern of sacred marriage between Goddess and king, the early Swedish kings all married an equivalent of Freya.

Crones

Morrigan *("Phantom queen," "washer at the ford," Insular Celtic)*

The Celtic Morrigan decided the fate of warriors. As they passed the ford, she would show them images of the ones fated to death. Sometimes she changed into a crow or a raven and hovered over the battlefield. She washed the blood from those who were slain and made magic from their blood. As *Macha*, she became a Goddess of both Life and Death. The dead went into her mounds, or barro-graves, where her tomb became the womb of rebirth, and their journey to the Otherworld began.

Durga *("Beyond reach," "demon slayer," Hindu)*

Durga is a female warrior, a destroyer of demons and monsters. Fierce and bloodthirsty, she rides her lion into battle. As Durga *Jagaddhatri*, she destroyed an army of giants. The head of the army of giants was named *Raktavija*. The Goddess wounded him, but from every drop of blood that flowed from his wounds, a thousand giants arose. Durga drank the giant's blood until only Raktavija remained. She killed him with one blow.

As Durga *Jagadgauri*, she is loved for saving both the immortals and humankind from demons. She is always triumphant. From the writings of *Yudhisthira* we read: "You are called Durga by all because you save us from difficulties, you are the sole refuge of humanity." Every year, Durga is honored as the slayer of the Buffalo Demon in a nine-day ritual called the *Durgapuja*. She is a destroyer Goddess as well as the one who saves the world from evil.

Urmya *("The night," Vedic Hindu)*

Urmya is the personification of the Night. She is kind and gentle. Her votaries are likened to birds who find repose by nesting in the trees. Urmya drives away wolves and thieves and keeps her votaries safe until the dawn.

Spider Grandmother *(Native American, Hopi)*

The story of Spider Grandmother tells us about the origin of the Four Worlds. The First World was inhabited by insects who lived in caves and were fond of fighting. Tawa, the Sun-Spirit, was not happy with them and so sent Spider Grandmother to take them all on a Journey of Changing. During their journey they were changed into dogs, wolves, and bears. This was the beginning of the Second World. But the creatures still did not understand life, and Tawa was thus not happy with them. Again he sent Spider Grandmother to teach them. She sent them on their next journey, in which they became people. Spider Grandmother told them to learn to live in harmony. This was the beginning of the Third World.

The people planted corn and built villages and Spider Grandmother taught them the arts of weaving and pottery. Although this was a better world, sorcerers started to turn people to evil ways. Then drought came and the corn crop failed.

Spider Grandmother returned and told the people with good hearts to leave the Third World and go to the Upper World. The people prayed and performed sacred ceremonies to find a way into the Upper World. They sent birds to find an opening in the sky. A swallow found an opening but the winds drove it back. A dove was sent and it flew though the opening. It found the new land but reported that there was no life there. They sent a hawk, but it came back with the same report. Then they sent a catbird, who found a deity called *Masauwa,* who said that the land was now ready and the people could come. The people were filled with joy, but then they realized they had no way to get there, as the Upper World was so high up.

Spider Grandmother suggested that a chipmunk help them get to the Upper World. The wise chipmunk planted trees so that the people could climb them and get into the Upper World. It planted a spruce, a fir-pine, and then a long-needle pine tree, but none of these trees grew high enough. Then the chipmunk planted a reed. Spider Grandmother instructed the people to sing so that the reed would grow high. It grew and grew until it grew through the opening in the sky.

Four lines were drawn on the ground by the chief and the wise men. It was decreed that if any sorcerer crossed the lines, it would mean his death. The people of good heart were able to cross over. Spider Grandmother led the climb up the reed and into the Upper World. The Fourth World is the Upper World, and this is the present world of the Hopi.

Hel *(Scandinavian)*

The Scandinavian Queen of the Underworld. Dead heroes who went to the house of Hel were called "Hel's men," or Helleder. Originally, Hel's place was probably an underground shrine or sacred cave of rebirth. The idea of a cauldron or womb filled with purifying fire may be related to a volcanic mountain. Hel was believed to be such a fire-mountain. In a German legend, the Emperor Theodoric became immortal by entering her womb through a volcano. "Burning Hel" was the name of the leader of the Valkyries, Brunnhilde. Hel was said to have received her underground realm from Odin. She had a great palace there, which was not a place of terror but merely the abode of the dead where even the Gods eventually arrived. Hel's underground depths were sometimes envisioned to be icy cold instead of filled with fire.

During the Middle Ages, her name remained as Frau Holde or Dame Holle, guardian of pagan souls, such as children who died unbaptized. It was also said that all children were birthed from "Dame Holle's Pond," which was the universal womb. The English word *hell* seems to have originated with the names for this Goddess, and subsequently took on the attributes of a place of torture and death.

Scadi *(Scandinavian)*

From the land of ice and snow, Scadi was called the Snow Shoe Goddess in the *Prose Edda* legends. She was a huntress, ranging the wilds for game. Scandinavia was named after her, for Scain-auja means the land of Scadi. A Goddess of shadow, she represented the Northern winter of cold and darkness, and was the one called upon for dark magic. Daughter of the giant Thjazi, she had a husband, Njord, a god of the seashore and ocean. She belonged in the high, mountainous uplands of her ancestors. After trying to live together for several days in one place or the other, they decided to return to their traditional homes.

Skalds, the poet-shamans of the north, probably received their name from Skadi, as a Goddess of inspiration. Believed to have the power to prophesy through their songs, they addressed the death goddess in funerary ballads. The *Eddas* were collections of anonymous poems that preserve the myth of the northern peoples, some dating from before the introduction of Christianity into Scandinavia. The name *Edda* seems to be connected to the word *great grandmother*, possibly making the legends "tales of a grandmother." The *Voluspa*, or *Prophesy of the Seeress*, is part of the *Verse Edda* and tells of the destruction of the Gods, to be followed by the resurgence of new gods and people in a new universe.

Circe *(Greek)*

A crone goddess of Greece associated with the moon. Her name is connected to "circle," and she was a spinner of fate and its cycles. Her sacred bird was the hunting falcon, *kirkos*. The island of Aeaea was her funerary shrine. Circe was also associated with sexual rites, and this was probably the source of Homer's description in the *Odyssey* of the witch who used her magic potions to turn all male visitors to swine. Patriarchal interpretations derided such sacred sexual rituals as releasing animal instincts. Odysseus was the only exception, because he was protected by Hermes, ruler of enlightened thought, who gave him a magic herb. One of Circe's symbols was the cauldron, a circular vessel, relating her to later Celtic lore.

Triune Goddesses

Brigit *("Bride," "high one," "the three mothers," "the three blessed ladies," Celtic)*

Brigit is the Triune Goddess of the Celts, representing the three primary crafts of Celtic society: poetry, healing, and smith-craft. Like some of the Greek muses, she was the inspiration of poets and bards, presiding over epics as well as rhymes and musical language.

Celtic myths give us the lovely image that flowers sprang up where the Goddess Brigit walked. Brigit kept cows ready with milk and never dry, and she governed an eternal spring. She is a Goddess of childbirth and also heals disease. In this aspect she is associated with wells whose waters are sacred in her name. She was popular not only in Ireland but in Northern Britain with the *Brigantes*.

Brigit remains in Christian lore, as Saint Brigid, the patron saint of animal husbandry and of the fertility of the land. February 1 is the Pagan holiday of Imbolc, an early spring fertility holiday of the Celts. Today in rural Ireland, grain and straw from last year's harvest are made into a Grain Dolly (fertility Goddess image). It is hung in houses, or in cottage thatch, and is set on the fields at St. Brigit's day. Grain is offered to the "saint" and cakes are set outside to feed hungry travelers.

Whether the Goddess is presented as the primary deity of the Pagan holiday of Imbolc or as the focus of the holiday of St. Brigit, it is the Goddess that is still being called upon. She is needed to make the lands fertile for the coming planting season. The message is the same: Wherever human beings have lived, they yearned for and needed the blessings of the Great Mother.

Moirai (*Greek*)

The Moirai were the three fates of Greek myth. Their name, which means "portion" or "share," refers to the measure of life given to every individual. The trio are called *Clotho*—the spinner, *Lachesis*—the measurer, and *Atropos*—the cutter. The myth is based in the idea of the weaver who creates destiny for people and Gods. Their lives are mystical threads spun by the Maiden, measured by the Mother, and finally cut by the Crone.

Graeae (*Greek*)

The Graeae or "Gray Ones," were another form of the three fates and seem to be a variation on the Moirai. Perseus is sent to cut off the head of Medusa but must ask the three Gray Ones where to find the grove of the Nymphs. The three have only one eye and one tooth between them, and he steals these to blackmail them into giving him the information. Then he throws the eye and tooth into Lake Triton to break their power. The Graeae were known as the Phorcides, or daughters of Phorcus, and were said to take on the form of cranes or swans, sacred birds. The prophetic three had the power to take omens from the flight of birds and to understand the secrets of the alphabet represented by cranes (who fly in "V" formation). Some mythographers give them credit for inventing the first alphabet.

Erinnyes (*Greek*)

The *Erinnyes* were deities of the underworld who had the special duty of punishing parricides and those who violated their oaths. Their names were *Tisiphone*, *Megara*, and *Alecto*. They probably first arose in Arcadia, where a Demeter Erinnyes was worshiped. They were called "Daughters of the Earth and the Shadow" by Sophocles and "the children of Eternal Night" by Aeschylus. Hesiod said they were fertilized by the blood of Uranus and born to Gaea. They were also called "the dogs of Hades." When a family crime was committed, they would appear armed with torches and whips and sit at the threshold of the house of the guilty, pursuing vengeance.

Moon Trinity (*Greek*)

Artemis, *Selene*, and *Hecate* formed a moon trinity, representing its three phases. Artemis was the virginal maiden goddess, a form of the "Lady of the Beasts" who lived in wild places. Selene, Goddess of the full moon, pulls the moon across the sky in her chariot. She was visualized as a cow and wore the horns of consecration, which formed crescent moons. Hecate, the crone of the trinity, was sacred to the waning and dark moon. She was associated with the ghosts of the underworld and was a mistress of magic. Her relation to the underworld also made her a deity of resurrection. In a depiction on the Mycenaean "Ring of Nestor" (1500 B.C.E.), she beckons celebrants from below to a transformation through the Goddess. Carved in the gold is a Cretan ritual around the Tree of Eternal Life. A worshiping couple follows the

Goddess, while above her head are seen two cocoons and two butterflies, symbols of transformation.

Capitoline Trinity *(Roman)*
The original female *Capitoline Triad* was *Juventas, Juno,* and *Minerva*—maiden, mother and crone. Capitoline refers to a temple on Rome's Capitoline Hill. Juno was Rome's Great Mother (see page 39).

Fortuna *(Roman)*
Fortuna was sometimes one goddess, but frequently known as the triple goddess *Fata Scribunda,* the Fate Who Writes. Her triad was a patron of fighters and gamblers and was associated with luck and good fortune.

Norns *(Scandinavian)*
Under the great ash tree, *Yggdrasill,* known as the spring of destiny or Fate, was the Well of Urd, the place where the Gods met in council each day. It was guarded by three Norns, the Germanic Goddesses of destiny. They were called *Urd* (fate), *Skuld* (being or becoming), and *Verdandi* (representing duty, a fateful debt, law, and necessity). The Norns protect and sustain the tree, which cares for all living creatures and the Gods who are guardians of man. Snorri Sturluson, whose *Prose Edda* (1220 B.C.E.) is a cornerstone work on Norse mythology, wrote: "It is said further that the Norns who live near the spring of Urd draw water from the spring every day, and along with it the clay that lies round about the spring, and they besprinkle the ash so that its branches shall not wither or decay."

In the thirteenth century, most believed that the Norns represented the three determining factors of their lives. *The Voluspa,* or *The Sibyl's Prophecy,* which dates from the ninth century, says about the Norns: "From there came three women, great knowledge they had. . . . They carve the stones, they determine the fates of human children, the length of their lives." Until the twentieth century, folk beliefs still existed about the Norns and their powers to exert influence over all human beings. Often related to the birth goddess, who controls the fate of a child, the three are akin to the old women in fairy tales who come to bestow qualities on the young princess.

The great tree Yggdrasill had three levels: Asgard, Midgard, and Niflheim. It was at Asgard that the Norns met. The symbol of three cosmic regions is found in Vedic Indian and Chinese mythologies. Shamanistic religions frequently also include the concept of several levels of worlds. Such ideas are found in many locations, an indication of their primal quality.

The Norns, or Nornir, probably originated from an Indo-European source. Associated with the moon, they always wear white. Each night the moon replaces the Sky Father (sun) with her three aspects: the crescent (Urd), the full moon (Verdandi), and the waning moon (Skuld). The Anglo-Saxon race believed in the power of the oldest sister Urd—at least until Shakespeare's time. Urd takes on the form Wyrd in Old English and means "fate," the destiny that no man or God escapes. The word is used nine times in the epic poem *Beowulf.* It is found in the chant of *Macbeth*'s Weird (Wyrd) Sisters, the three witches who gathered around their cauldron on a barren heath, intoning: "Fair is foul and foul is fair. Hover through the fog and filthy air." They were predicting the future for the unfortunate hero of the play.

Urd may have been the original single Norn, and in that phase was Mother Earth, or Ertha. Skuld, the death Norn, was a variation of the goddess Skadi. She was also known as one of the Valkyries, who chose the slain in battlefields for the pleasant afterlife of Valhalla.

4

The Crone Connection to Goddesses Dark, Wise, and Magical

—M.H.

The Crone is a mistress of arts that are dark, wise, and magical. In her magic place of ritual and transformation, she approaches the wondrous elements all around her. Finding exotic, lovely things to bring into being, she enjoys the fruits of her labors. When healing and freedom from fear is needed, she can be there. When the world is out of balance, she bends her wise judgment to bring it back. Out of her cauldron, she creates all that is useful or fantastic to make life sweet.

Crone goddesses, those who personify later life, are known for their predominance in the three areas: darkness, wisdom, and magic. The Dark traits of a Goddess have to do with the mysteries of death and rebirth, for traditionally the Crone presided over both these important transitions. Wisdom is another quality for which women in their later years are revered. The Crone's wisdom is the result of living for many decades and having the advantage of experience acquired along the way. The use of Magic can be another form of wisdom. It is particularly important when it is embodied in the Crone, for greater power can be attained in the years of Wise Blood.

The Dark Goddess

Dark Goddesses have been among us at least since Neolithic times (7000 B.C.E. to 3000 B.C.E.). They were found in Neolithic Europe and Anatolia, where they presided over the rites of death and were believed to facilitate rebirth. The Bird Goddess of these times appeared both as a giver of life and well-being and as death in the form of the vulture or the owl—birds of prey and carrion eaters. Bird Goddess figurines in clay and rock carvings usually had a long body and a face which might represent a mask, with a beaklike nose and eyes. There was usually no mouth. The bird Goddess's sacred animal was the ram, and ram horns are often depicted in grave and funerary ceramics. The Greek Athena seems to be a descendant of the prehistoric bird Goddesses. She received sacrifices of rams as her sacred animal. She is often associated with birds such as the owl, vulture, duck, swallow, and dove.

The image of the snake was connected with cycles of death and rebirth because it repeatedly shed its skin and because it lived in the earth and hibernated. In her poisonous aspect, the Dark Goddess was the Goddess of Death. The Later Indo-European, Semitic, and Christian beliefs depicted the snake as evil; yet other peoples thought the snake assured well-being and harmony with the cycles of nature. The Snake Goddess was also important as an image of vitality, especially the life energy of the home. It was believed until quite recently in Lithuania that killing a green housesnake results in the death of a family member.

The White Goddess of death and resurrection was often depicted in the stiff nudes sculpted of bone or marble at burial sites in the Aegean and Mediterranean. White is the color of bones. Masks of this Goddess do not have a mouth, only the large nose of the Bird Goddess. The Great Goddess of the Stone Age represented a repeating cycle that underlies all her manifestations. Therefore, images of death incorporated images of birth. Tombs in Sardinia and temple chambers in Malta are eggshaped, ready to hatch new life. Other symbols of the womb and regeneration are the frog, the hedgehog, the butterfly, and the bull's head, which, with its two horns, is shaped like a uterus. At Catal Huyuk (7th millennium

B.C.E.), a temple above graves was decorated with paintings and reliefs signifying death in the form of the vulture and regeneration in the form of the frog. Many bull heads were shown, some with nourishing breasts above them. The symbolism plainly shows a concern with the forces of birth and regeneration. Other symbols of life stimulation in these chambers were triangles, honeycombs, chrysalises and butterflies, vulvas, phalluses, and water, which stood for amniotic fluids.

Fairy tales, customs, and language show that the image of the Death Goddess has survived to this day. There are Germanic tales of Frau Holla, an old hag with a long nose and large teeth. She controls snow and the regeneration of nature. She appears as a dove in the spring to ensure fertility. She is also Holla who comes from the inner depths of mounds and caves, her name being similar to *hohle,* meaning cave. The dead were supposed to live under the elder tree, which was called *holler* and had healing powers. The Russian Baba Yaga has a long hooked nose and lives in a house standing on bird's feet. In the Serbo-Croatian languages, *baba* is "old woman" and *yaga* is associated with sickness, fear, and wrath, relating to the Death Goddess.

The Old Irish tradition has a Death Goddess called Ana, also known as Anu and Danu. She was mother of the dead and presided over regeneration. Her nourishing quality gave its name to a pair of hills in County Kerry called "the Paps of Anu." This is a reflection of similar thinking during the Megalithic era, when breasts were sculptured on tomb walls.

Many cultures have goddesses of death and resurrection. The Greek Persephone descends into the underworld to care for the dead. In China, Meng-Po Niang-Niang was the Goddess of hell and reincarnation. Her house was just inside the exit to Hell, where she brewed the Broth of Oblivion, which stopped a reincarnating person from remembering past lives. Hikuleo was Goddess of the underworld in Hawaii. Pele ruled over volcanoes as well as the underworld. Among the Mayas, Masaya was the Goddess of death and volcanoes. Among the Pueblo Indians in North America, Iyatiku was a corn Goddess who lived in the underworld. In Africa, Ala, or Ane, was Queen of the Dead and the harvest, and Asase Yaa created life and also received the dead.

The takeover of the lands of the Old European peoples by the Indo-Europeans created a hybrid of the two belief structures. The patriarchal Indo-Europeans did not see life as a cycle of birth and death in the same way Goddess-oriented groups did, but understood death as an ending with no return. Therefore, the death Goddess was much to be feared. The primal dark Goddess of India was Kali, who was transformed through time into other Goddesses. Originally, Kali was creator of the universe, of primordial energy. She brought everything into being and then destroyed it so she could create again, since everything was cyclical. Although a Triple Goddess, she is known mainly for her aspect as destroyer. The Hindu Kali was black because she represented darkness at both the beginning and end of life. She was also Mother Night, who gave birth to Love, Fate, Nemesis, Sleep, and Death. In her Crone aspect, she represented both the tomb and the womb.

Because the Indo-Europeans, over centuries, made their way from Asia and India, and traveled as far as Scandinavia and the British Isles, Kali was probably the base name for the *Caillech*, who gave the name Caledonia to Scotland. Her name means old woman, hag, and veiled one and refers to her abilities to know the future, particularly the time of death. A medieval legend speaks of her as the Black Queen of a western land the Spaniards named *Califia*, source of the word California.

Patriarchal religions, such as that of the Indo-Europeans and later the Judaic, Islamic, and Christian theologies, divided women into those who were either nurturing or destructive to men. Women existed to take care of men's needs, so any independence or power was considered destructive unless under male control. Men viewed women as either the virgin, the mother or the whore, the good woman or the evil witch. The female icon desired by such men was an ever-loving and ever attentive young mother, beautiful and complaisant. The other aspects of Mother, Maiden, and Crone in women were not considered and frequently labeled evil, including the concept of the Sex-Goddess-Temptress and the Crone-Witch.

The opposite of the nourishing mother figure was the Crone. A patriarchal culture might tolerate women who have grown older, but any independent abilities or latent powers were thought to be more harmful than useful. However, as the Indo-Europeans progressed into Europe and Asia, a combining of the patriarchal and matriarchal developed. Many female deities were consorts of the Gods, less powerful but with recognized importance. Yet the Crone was frequently seen as witch, sorceress, succubus, Hag, Night-mare, or she-demon.

In Ireland, the Celtic Morrigan was a Goddess of war. Her aspect was the crow or raven who flapped her wings against the window of people about to die. Like a vulture, she was a feeder on corpses in battlefields. The Scandinavian Mother Night birthed the three Norns. Their underworld was called the land of Scath, another name for Scadi, which literally means shadow or shade. Although the Egyptians were not considered influenced by the Indo-Europeans, they had Nut or Neith. Out of her womb, the sun arose and then returned at night.

The powers of the Dark Goddess can be awesome, and we have to be very sure of our purposes when we work with her, for she is death, the fear that dwells with us all. But as we get older, we must acknowledge her and consider her a friend. She can be an inspiration to make the best use of our lives, for we know that our time is not endless. The saying "never put off until tomorrow what you can do today" may have been coined by her, for if we are wise, we eventually learn that today is all we have. Crones who understand this gain a great amount of serenity and patience. They make a point of accomplishing their goals without pushing things off in a corner and saying, "I'll come back to that some day." Take the time to enjoy your life and go after what you want. Later on you may not be around.

Crones are the traditional caretakers of the ill and the dying. When they are in their fifties, their parents may be in their seventies and eighties and may have illnesses that will result in death. These parents' children, now Crones, will be the ones most likely to take care of them. This may not be an easy time, but it calls for the abilities of compassion to raise the spirits and to heal or ease the pain. The Crone does this not only for her family members but for others as well, for she knows that all life ends in death, and her business is to help others who may not have the benefit of her understanding.

The Wise Goddess

The wisdom of women, especially older women, has always been a quality for which they were known. Although many times negated through the centuries, it is still the basis of many beliefs and customs. Having innate wisdom and the benefit of life experience, the Crone is the wisest of all. She is said to have Wise Blood. It was believed that even after menopause, menses were retained within as a source of power and magical purpose. The phenomenon of Wise Blood made old women the wisest of all human beings. In Christian Europe, until the seventeenth century, descriptions of witches asserted that their magic powers came from the retention of lunar blood within their bodies.

As the tribal Mothers and Grandmothers made rules to guide the behavior of their children and matristic clans, so they handed down laws and justice to the tribe. "She openeth her mouth with wisdom; and in her tongue is the law of kindness," says the Bible (Prov. 31:26). Since early times, women formulated rules of good behavior. Female tribal elders were believed to understand religious and magical lore, including the knowledge of good and evil. The Goddess Tiamat gave her sacred tablets of law to her first son, Kingu, whose blood was said to form the first man. Rhea, Goddess of Crete, gave her tablets of law to the original King Minos at her temple on Mount Dicte. The Tablets of Law that Moses received from the mountain God were probably copies of earlier tablets of law, said to be received from the Goddess herself.

In pre-Roman times, Ceres Legifera, or Ceres the Lawgiver, dispensed *ius naturale,* or the "natural law," which was their legal system. Even the classical, male-oriented, patriarchal Greeks and Romans attributed the basis of their law codes to Mother Goddesses such as Demeter or Ceres, both Goddesses of grain and harvest.

One of the oldest Goddesses in Egypt was Heqit, or Hekat, a name derived from the root *heq,* which means intelligence. Another form of this deity was the Greek Hecate, the Crone form of the Mother Goddess Hera. The Heq was a tribal leader, called the Divine Grandmother, who bore the flail, the symbol of authority. Her words of power, or *hekau*, commanded all things, including forces of creation and destruction. Dynastic Egyptians subscribed to the laws of Maat, Mother Goddess of Truth. Maat presided over justice, deciding the ultimate fate of Egyptians at death by weighing their souls in her balances.

The Hebrew Hokmah, meaning "maternal wisdom," may have come from a combination of Hekat and Maa, Hek-Maa. In *The Wisdom of Solomon*, Hokmah is called the all-powerful Mother and creator of all things. When the Greeks translated the Bible, her name became Sophia, or Wisdom. Proverbs 8 of the Bible refers to the spirit of Hokmah as God's co-creator. However, the Bible contradicts the idea in Proverbs 9, which ridicules the Goddess Hokmah and her priestesses. Later, male scholars overlooked or eliminated any further allusions to feminine wisdom.

The Koreshites, children of the Goddess Kore, were residents of Mecca and ancestors of Muhammed. They were guardians of the sacred Black Stone and worshiped a deity called the Old Woman. The Black Stone was marked by a female genital sign and covered by a veil representing the veiled future. Arabia had a matriarchal culture for more than a thousand years before the advent of Islam. Her primary Goddess was a trinity sometimes called Al-lat. The original parts of the Muslim Koran existed many centuries before the time of Muhammed. Legends say it was copied from a divine tablet that appeared in heaven at the beginning of eternity called "Mother of the Book." It was transcribed by holy *imams*, wise ones, whose name relates to the Semitic word *ima*, mother. Today, the Black Stone of Mecca reposes in the Kaaba, the holiest shrine of Islam.

Among the Northern Germanic tribes, sagas are written histories originally created by female priestesses and poets. Saga means "female sage" or "omniscience." One of the names of the Great Goddess, it was also applied to the heroic epics of the Scandinavians. The sagas of the northern tribes were mainly written by women, who knew how to read and write the runes. Every saga, which was sung to an audience, began with an invocation to Erda or Earth, the primal grandmother. Jacob Grimm suggests that, in ancient poems like the *Rigspula*, *edda* meant tales of the grandmother. The *eddas* were an important source of the history and tradition of the North, dating back before the introduction of Christianity into Scandinavia. They were the songs of the Skalds or sages of Norway, Denmark, Iceland and Sweden. In the Norse creation story, Edda was the first woman to produce offspring with her husband Ai.

Themis, daughter of Gaia, was the most hallowed of Greek Goddesses. She is shown holding a pair of scales and a cornucopia. Themis determined the seasons and the time of growth and blossoming. She came to signify the social contract among people living on the earth. In this, she exemplified the power of convention, or what is fixed, steadfast, and right, even as there is a proper moment for fruitful growth. All society looked to her wisdom. No Olympian gathering could take place unless she called it, and no God could lift a cup of nectar until she had drunk.

By inquiring into the sources of the tribal wisdom of many cultures, the work of women, and most especially the Crones, or elders, is seen to have produced many of the founding precepts. The Crone is an adviser to rulers and can see clearly the past, present, and future. Her wisdom has thus been instrumental in guidance and the upholding of law.

We are all born with certain wisdom, but in the Crone this wisdom emerges full-blown, for it has been nourished by the residue of experience. If a Crone has particular interests, she has had the time to study and work on these interests in depth. She has been taught and now has the ability, even the duty, to teach others her knowledge, for it has always been important to pass on the knowledge of the human race. Crones are mature enough to understand when there is a deep and important need, something that should be practiced and brought to fulfillment, or when an idea is a passing fancy, a superficial one that may only impede her progress. That's why the Crone might find herself changing jobs or occupations in middle age, or suddenly taking up painting, when the only art she had previously done was doodling on an inter-office memo.

When a woman has reached Cronehood, she may become an expert and icon in the field she pursues. Others can see her importance, how much she contributed. People flock to Crones to learn answers to their questions, as one would come to a renowned doctor for a second opinion. The Crone may write her wisdom in a book or tell it to her grandchildren. Whatever she does, she knows the importance of using her powers wisely.

The Magical Goddess

The use of magic to influence life is found in cultures throughout the world, and the Crone is frequently the source of magical methods. The Greek Hecate and the Celtic Irish Cerridwen are both known for their magical adventures. There are others connected with deeds of magic, some famous and others as obscure as the Celtic goddess Agsagsona, a being of the underworld who is invoked as a weaver of spells.

Morrigan was a Triple Goddess who presided at battles and could influence them as she wished. In one capacity, she is a Goddess of death and resurrection. She makes magic by singing runes and casting charms. The Arthurian Morgan le Fay is probably a later incarnation of this Goddess. *Mor* means "sea" in the Celtic language, and Morgan the Sea Goddess still survives in tales from Brittany. In Welsh mythology, *Le Fay* means "the fairy," but it may also mean "the fate." She was associated with the magic of fairies and was called Queen of Avalon by the Welsh—Avalon being the underworld place where King Arthur went after he disappeared from earth.

The Yoruban goddess Oya of Africa presides over wind, storms, and change. She comes from around the Niger River, arriving in the New World with the African slaves. She is found in Brazil, where she is called Yansa. Among those who practice voodoo in Haiti and New Orleans she is Aida-Wedo. She is also seen as a warrior Goddess who lives in the whirlwind. The magic of transformation is one of her specialties. Her magic can help you fight a battle, change old things, or create something new. Mirror magic and prophecy are part of her tradition.

The Greek sorceress Pamphile was adept at metamorphosis. She could change her shape by rubbing herself with ointment by the light of her magic lamp. She often became an owl, the Crone's bird, flying through the night to bathe in spring water and then returning to human form in the daytime.

Freya, of the Norse myths, was the leader of the female deities known as Divine Matriarchs, who ruled the clans before the Indo-European Aesir took over. As Syr she was a seer and the death-sow. Her magic or witchcraft was known as seidr and was shamanistic, represented by her cape of falcon feathers. She could shape-shift into a bird or descend to the underworld and return with prophecies. Magic, trance, and divination were aspects of seidr, considered a feminine mystical craft. The word shaman or *saman* comes from the Tungus people of Siberia. It means a healer or individual with special spiritual powers, which can be considered magical. The shaman is found throughout the world, including Japan, North and South America, and Polynesia.

Among the Celtic peoples of Ireland, *Ollamh* is the name traditionally given to the shaman of the Fairy Wicca tradition. These shamans were most often older women who knew the healing arts based on herb craft and other ancient practices, including word vibration, chanting, charms, and magical ceremonials. The Ollamh was believed to be able to use charms or spells to heal or to kill, as he or she wished. One of the traits of the Ollamh is the ability to enter an altered state at will, connecting mind, body, and spirit to understand hidden realities. The Fairy tradition stems from the Tuatha De Danann, or people of the Goddess Dana. She is considered the primal Goddess and may have been associated with the River Don in Russia.

Magic, which is a "bending" of reality toward the purposes of the magician, is basically a practice of the spirit and may involve calling on deities. Wicca, which means "to bend," often includes magic or ceremonies for special purposes. In its mundane form, magic may influence everyday life, such as in blessing a home. It might concern the acquisition of something most desired—a car, a job, a lover. On a more universal scale, it may be a request for wealth, healing or good fortune. In any case, it involves the tuning in to other worlds, and thus the realm of the spirit and the Gods and Goddesses is involved.

The performance of magic is a tradition that requires wisdom and study. Knowledge must be gained and abilities must be honed. The Crone has had the benefit of experience and an understanding of people and life. She is the one traditionally considered a magician If she subscribes to a particular spiritual practice based in the Goddess, she may also be a priestess. Therefore, the magical Crone can be found in cultures worldwide.

The Crone magician has gathered within herself much magical knowledge and she knows how to use it. Protection spells, requests for luck, and other benefits are her province. She may be acquainted with esoteric magic or simple candle spells. She has mastered the basics of rituals, such as calling in the directions and knowing the properties of the elements: earth, air, fire, and water. She must be aware of magical tools and magical times and seasons, as well as moon phases.

Magic is a way of actively working with elements given by the One Who Creates and bringing about the manifestation of what is desired. Most important in the magician's work is her intent, for this is the power behind the magic. Yet she subscribes to the precept, "Do what you will, ere you harm none." The Crone believes in the mysterious force of magic and doesn't mind asking for what she wants. In all she accomplishes, the Crone enjoys communing with the elements and powers through her magical work, and she cherishes the results.

5

The Symbols of
the Crone

—J.R. & M.H.

A symbol is a powerful tool, evoking magical mental images. Symbols can stand for events, for people, for ideas. We quickly respond to symbols that are part of our culture. They may bring up many things, from tastes and smells to hopes and fears. A symbol can come across in the written word, an image, or even a gesture. Raising the hands in a certain way can be a symbol for blessing. The dove is a symbol for peace. Symbols have the impact of images combined with the substance of our thoughts. When we are doing personal work or participating in a ritual, a symbol can help us to get into the deep places of meaning.

Symbols have been used by the very earliest cultures known to us. They are part of the way we communicate with each other. They can carry inner significance, both psychological and spiritual. A picture of a bee may show that there is a bee hive in the area, or it many mean that someone is busy as a bee. It also may have a deeper significance. In ancient Greece, certain priestesses of the Goddess were called *melissae,* or bees.

The Crone has her special symbols, and these can be utilized in various ways. They are drawn from the natural world and myth. Their meanings are not only affected by their placement within a myth, but by their purpose or their practical use as an object. A symbol conveys layers of meaning, connecting to our psyches and the unconscious mind much the way dreams do. Their interpretation gives us a view of these layers. Sometimes symbols have a special meaning to an individual because of personal history and experience.

Some symbolic meanings are unique to a cultural context, such as the "blue cauldron" of the ancient Babylonian Goddess Seris. Other symbols have the same meaning in many cultures, like the cauldron image, which can represent both womb and tomb. In this chapter, we will examine some of the symbols—both familiar and unfamiliar—associated with the Crone.

Cauldron

The cauldron is a place where things are boiled down to their usable essence and then transformed into something that can sustain life. The cauldron is activated by fire. The fiery heat below the cauldron changes living things into food, which can then support life. The metaphor is that death sustains life through the vehicle of the cauldron. This is the source of the primary magical quality of the cauldron, as a tool of transformation that promotes life.

The physical shape of the cauldron and of many ancient vessels and pots is likened to a womb. Its form is the feminine container for creation. The womb and woman are deeply connected with the magical powers of the cauldron. Further, the blackness of an old iron cauldron, aged by use in magical processes, connects it more specifically with the Crone aspect of the Triple Goddess.

Medeia, the Greek enchantress, could rejuvenate those who were old by boiling a magic brew in her cauldron with certain herbs. Her cauldron was pictured as a large round metal bowl suspended by a tripod, below which burned a fire. There is an image of her rejuvenating an old ram in this way, painted on a water jar from Vulci, dated 475 B.C.E. (from Cavendish, *Mythology: An Illustrated Encyclopedia*).

The Babylonian Goddess Siris, a Goddess of the Stars, had under her command the whole of the blue heavens where she stirred the drink of regeneration. Representations of her cauldron were made out of the blue stone lapis lazuli.

In Welsh mythology, the magical Cauldron of Rebirth brings dead soldiers back to life. It also provides a continuous supply of food and can make those who eat the food immortal. The well-known Gundestrup Cauldron of the Celts was found in Denmark, and dates to the second century B.C.E. Aside from the fertility God Cernunnos being portrayed on its exterior surface, there is also a picture of a figure placing slain warriors into a cauldron-like vessel.

Owl

It is the mythical wisdom of the owl, combined with its nocturnal activities, that links it to the Crone. Its ability to see its prey through the dark of night demonstrates its vision when others cannot see. Its all-knowing eyes, large and wide, convey not only keen sight but a kind of natural awareness. The movement of its head, almost all the way around, makes the owl appear strange and unearthly.

The Etruscans, and later the Romans, used the activities and movements of birds for divination. The name for Italian witches, or wise women, came to be *Strega*. Strega traces back to the Latin word for owl, which is *strix*, the plural being *streges*. Romans gave a negative connotation to the sighting of an owl, viewing it as the herald of disaster. The Roman author Horace wrote that witches used owl feathers in their magical brews.

The owl was a symbol of wisdom for the Greek Goddess Athena, and became one of her emblems. Also, according to author Barbara Walker in *The Women's Encyclopedia of Myths and Secrets,* the owl was also called a "night-hag" in the medieval period, when this bird was thought to be a witch who shape-shifted into the form of an owl.

Raven

Ravens, like crows, are scavengers. They are associated with death because they hover over the battlefield awaiting the falling of dead warriors. Among the Celts, the raven was the totem of the Goddess Morrigan, who helped bring slain warriors over to "the Otherside." The Nordic Valkyries were death Goddesses who, in raven-form or wearing black raven feathers, drank the blood of slain warriors and then took their souls to Valhalla, to heaven.

Among the natives of Alaska and Siberia, the raven is a primary God who is wedded to the Great Mother. Their raven sacrificed itself to bring magic to humankind. Among Native Americans of the Northwest coast, the raven is a trickster God who drives others off from stores of food with its tricks and magical powers. One story is that the raven brought stars to the night sky by stealing a bag of stars (which was a toy for a chief's daughter) and then throwing it up through the tepee smoke-hole, thereby scattering its contents across the sky. In addition, for these indigenous peoples of the far northern hemisphere, it is the raven who established the laws that govern earth.

Scythe

The scythe has a dual meaning, being connected both to the Mother Goddess and to the Crone. It is by the power of the scythe that the abundance of the Mother is gathered in. At the same time, it is the cutting action of the scythe that ends the lives of plants in the field and leaves the field barren.

As a reaper, the wielder of the scythe was a Death Goddess. She stemmed from a Scythian Goddess (Scythia was a part of the Ukraine, once inhabited by nomadic horse warrior tribes), who was called Rhea Cronia by the Greeks. She was also called Mother Time. During the medieval period, she was changed to the Grim Reaper, a male image who used a scythe to bring death. In the Greek Mysteries of Demeter, it is Hecate who wields a scythe, and thereby separates the Maiden grain plants from Mother Earth, turning the Maiden into Persephone (Goddess of the Land of Death).

The scythe, with its cutting blade, is a symbol of the power to separate one element from another. Its blade gathers in life, but also begets death. The scythe is an image of the power to create major life transitions. It marks time with these transitions and is valuable as a Crone tool for cutting away what one does not want. Its power to banish things is an important aspect, as we must create endings to make way for new things in our lives.

Dark Moon

The symbol of the black disc is used in astronomy and astrology to convey that portion of the lunar cycle when the moon is not visible in the night sky. At those times, Earth is so positioned to prevent the light of the sun from being projected onto the moon's surface. The soft, silvery lunar light is then held away from our portion of the earth. This phase of the moon and the absence of lunar light have an effect on earthly life. It is a time of low energy, the opposite of the time of the full moon, when life is greatly stimulated by lunar influences.

The black disk, as the symbol of the dark moon, can be a general symbol for the Dark Goddess. It conveys the aspects of death, barrenness, and endings. It can also symbolize a time of quiet, a fallow period in which activity ceases so that regeneration and preparation for the next creative cycle can begin. The dark moon represents the darkness of the womb, a black cavern full of expectation. This is the sacred pause, the moment in time when, like the blackness of space, the Dark Goddess rests before giving birth to a universe of stars.

Snake

The snake as a symbol is known throughout the world. It lives inside the earth and therefore is in direct contact with the source of our existence. Snakes, who come from the womb of Mother Earth, were alleged to possess all wisdom because they were in contact with the Wise Blood of the world. This was the source of knowledge to predict the future and give advice attributed to the oracular serpent Python at Delphi in Greece. (The oracular priestess at Delphi was called the Pythoness.)

Another attribute of the snake is that it grows by shedding its skin, and so can be a symbol of regeneration. When it hibernates, it simulates death. The Neolithic Snake Goddess image showed snakelike hands and feet, a snake-shaped head, and a wide mouth. Horns or moon crescents also were associated with snakes and were found on these reptiles in Paleolithic cave drawings. It is probable these had to do with powers of regeneration. As one living within the earth, the snake was also a symbol of life energy. The snakes who guarded Greek homes were called the *Zeus Ktesios*, and in Rome they were known as *penates dii*.

Crete is well known for images of the Goddess and her sacred priestesses. Sculptures show the goddess holding a snake in each hand, her breasts exposed and snakes encircling her waist and arms. The snakes of life and death were part of their beliefs, and in their temples they kept many snakes in special baskets and jars. The snake was also important to the Egyptians, for pharaohs wore the uraeus, a rearing cobra, on their forehead as part of their crowning headdress. The uraeus symbol is a hieroglyphic sign for "Goddess."

The Indo-Europeans, however, considered the snake a symbol of evil, an epiphany of the God of death, lurking in the underworld and the whirlwind. In the Bible, the story of Adam and Eve features the serpent as the evil one who tempts Eve to eat the apple, prompting God to evict Adam and Eve from Eden.

Lamia was the Greek name for the serpent goddess of Libya. She was worshiped as a bringer of fertility and connected to the water of oases. Sinuous dances in her honor imitated the movements of a snake. Lamia may be a variation on the Babylonian Mother of Gods, Lamashtu, who was worshiped as a serpent with the head of a woman. She was also thought to be the Libyan Neith, a love and battle Goddess, related to Anatha and Athena, whose worship was suppressed by the Achaeans. A Greek legend tells that Lamia joined the company of the Empusae, lying with young men and sucking their blood while they slept. During the middle ages, Lamia became a term for a witch or demon in the shape of an old woman.

Until recently, according to archaeologist Marija Gimbutas, the Slavic peoples still believed in Domovoi, sometimes seen as a man and sometimes a snake, who protected their homes and well-being. The Lithuanians had a "Day of the Snakes" when they prepared food for snakes and invited them into their homes.

Prosperity for the year depended on whether the snakes ate the food. In Ireland, February 1 is the holiday of Brigit, when the Queen returns from the hills. The Queen was a snake Goddess who ruled over all the other snakes. Interestingly enough, it is believed in European folklore that whoever holds the Queen's crown will know all the secrets of the world and understand the speech of animals.

The snake is a powerful symbol. To make a snake your friend, treat it as a wise companion, a protector who can impart its wisdom and oracular knowledge if you need it. Consider the beauty of its shape, a sacred spiral or a curl, which forms part of many significant designs. Snakes symbolize both death and regeneration but when they have symbolized only death, they were often considered evil. The snake is a protector, especially a protector of homes. Among the Egyptians, it was a symbol of royalty. The snake can be an emblem of slyness or covertness, but above all it is a symbol of knowledge and the understanding of nature's secrets.

Frog

The frog, which transforms from a tadpole, was also a symbol of regeneration. Gimbutas mentions a stone amulet in the shape of a frog-woman from her archaeological site at Achilleion, Thessaly (6300–6200 B.C.E.). At the excavation of Catal Huyuk, the Goddess was represented on wall paintings in two forms: vultures, who signify death, and frogs, who represent regeneration. The frog was seen as a kind of "traveling womb" because of its shape.

To Egyptians, the frog was associated with birth-magic and symbolized the fetus. The Goddess Hekat, Queen of Heavenly Midwives, had a sacred Amulet of the Frog that carried the words, "I Am the Resurrection." Witches in the middle ages had frog totems because frogs were long associated with Hecate.

In German folk tales, the old Hag, Goddess of winter, is Holla, who controls the appearance of the sun, of snow, and the regeneration of nature. To ensure fertility, she appears once a year as a dove. In the spring, she is a frog who brings the red apple that symbolizes life back to earth from the well where it fell at harvest time.

The frog can indicate growth, regeneration, birth, and even romance. Sometimes it has its humorous aspect, but it is a unique and versatile symbol that is at home on both water and earth.

Cat

The cat has many identities in many cultures. It has been seen as a form of divinity and a form of evil. In different places, it has symbolized the sun or the moon, light and darkness, religion or dark magic.

In Egypt, the cat was of great importance and at one time probably symbolized the Great Mother. The Cat Goddess was known in two forms. Sekhmet had a lion's head and was a warrior Goddess who represented the harsh, destructive aspects of the sun. Bast was the warming, generative aspects of the sun, a Goddess of love, music, and the arts as well as a bringer of good fortune. Frequently she is seen carrying the *sistrum,* a sacred musical instrument often adorned with the image of a cat. Bast was also seen as a moon Goddess, who, with her reflective eyes, held the light of the sun safely during the night. After the Egyptians, the cat was invoked in Rome and Europe as the moon Goddess Isis.

In an ancient Egyptian myth, Atet, the Mother Goddess, took the form of a cat to slay Apep, the serpent of darkness. Later, the slaying of the serpent was attributed to the god Ra, personification of the life-giving properties of the sun, who also took the form of a cat. The Egyptian word for cat is *mau,* which points to how it became a symbol of day, or the sun God, because *mau* also means "light."

Cats were believed to be clairvoyant and to represent the transmission of thought. In the Finnish *Kalevala*, the magician Lemminkainen causes a group of men to be thrown into a sledge drawn by a cat. The cat takes them into the deserted areas of Lapland, where no horse can travel, to the very limits of Pohjola, the world of darkness and evil spirits, thus demonstrating the extent of his powers. Freya, Scandinavian Goddess of love, had a chariot drawn by cats. Being a Goddess of fertility, she helped the land to sprout and bloom. When farmers placed a pan of milk in the cornfields for her cats to drink, she was especially pleased, protecting their crops from bad weather and other problems.

Worship of the moon Goddess Diana was marked by Sabbats, or Sabbaths, occurring four times a year in celebration of the seasons. The moon was represented by the symbol of the cat, so the Romans often wore skins and masks to impersonate cats. During the middle ages, the Church identified such celebrants as witches, worshipers of the Devil.

Witches were often identified with cats. Sometimes they were said to ride on cats as well as broomsticks, or to turn themselves into cats. Isobel Gowdie, Queen of Scottish Witches, made a confession in 1662 that she and her group, or coven, had taken the form of cats, crows, and hares to roam through the countryside. Marie Lamont of Inverkip said that the Devil came to members of her coven and changed them into witches by shaking his hands above their heads. The result of such stories is that cats in countries where witches were persecuted were said to be their "familiars," and were also caught and killed in great numbers.

Cat legends are found throughout the world. The Oraons of Bengal believed that some women had the power to change their soul into a black cat. The Burmese and the Siamese still believe their sacred temple cats embody the spirits of the dead. Japan has temple cats, which are born with certain markings considered sacred. They are black and white with a spot on their backs and are said to contain the soul of an ancestor.

Cats are found in legends as genii, demons, or ghosts. Egyptians, Etruscans, and Indians portrayed them in Paradise. Being in touch with the other world, the cat was seen to have knowledge of the future and, more mundanely, to be able to foretell the weather, as in this old nursery rhyme:

> *If near the fire the kitten's back was found.*
> *Frost was at hand, and snows hung hovering round.*
> *Her paw prophetic raised above her ear*
> *Foretold a visit, for some friend was near.*

The cat is the quintessential symbol and companion for a witch. A versatile animal, it can symbolize the moon or the sun, or it can show intuition or clairvoyance. It may be seen as a sacred animal and can stand for a person's soul. There are ghost cats, demon cats, and cats that provide transportation and carry messages, possibly to or from another world.

Spider

The spider is prominent in the myths of Native America because of the Spider Woman. Among the Keresan Pueblos she is the supreme being. She is able to create everything by thinking, naming, dreaming, and chanting. Her other names are Grandmother Spider and Creating-Through-Thinking, or Thought Woman. Like many other groups, the Keresan have an origin myth. Iyatiku and her sister Nautssiti are sent by Spider Woman upwards from their world, emerging into the light on this earth. They bring with them baskets full of seeds and clay images from which they create all forms of life.

The Hopi Spider Woman helps during the emergence and is the mother of all. She has her own shrines and is a benevolent but stern guardian. The Jicarilla Apaches forbid the killing of spiders because they were the ones who helped the first beings to climb up during the emergence. Old Woman Spider helps monster-slayer escape.

In monster-slayer mythology, Spider Woman frequently helps, but sometimes will threaten the heroes of the myth. Spider Woman gave the Navajos their great gift as weavers, because of a Pueblo girl who lived among them. She wandered away from the village and discovered a hole in the ground with smoke coming out of it. It was Spider Woman's home. The girl was invited inside and taught how to weave. The girl returned, giving the knowledge of her new ability to the Navajo community. It is the custom of the Navaho to remember Spider Woman's gift by leaving a small hole in their blankets or other woven items to represent the entrance to Spider Woman's house.

According to Greek legend, Arachne was a priestess from Lydian Colophon, a region famed for its purple dyes. The Goddess Athena (Minerva) instructed her in weaving, and Arachne became famous for her beautiful creations. Out of vanity she challenged Athena to a competition in weaving. Both wove wonderful tapestries, but even Athena admitted that Arachne's was the best. Becoming enraged, Athena destroyed Arachne's tapestry and struck her with a spinning shuttle. Arachne was humiliated and attempted to hang herself, but Athena turned her into a spider, and ever since Arachnids have been famous for their splendid webs.

The spider was a totemic form of the Fate Spinner, also known as Clotho, Moera, or Athena. A Greek icon shows Athena with her spider totem as she spins the web of Fate, making it possible to foretell the future. It is often said that spiders can forecast the weather in folklore. In Scandinavian myth, Odin's horse, Sleipnir, had eight legs like a spider and was gray. He also represented Odin's Fate.

Maya, virgin aspect of the Triple Goddess, was represented in Hindu myth by a spider. Maya could become Kali-Uma, the death Goddess, when she was identified with the species of female spiders that devour their mates. In Aztec myths, spiders represented the souls of women warriors from pre-Aztec times.

The spider is first and foremost a symbol of weaving, and thus can also be a symbol of a creator. Spiders as weavers of fate are often portrayed in myth; thus the spider is identified with knowing and foretelling the future. Spiders as predators are patient catchers of insects in their webs. They can be small and delicate, but a few varieties, like the desert spider, have very large bodies. Some females actually eat their consorts after mating, creating fearful connotations. Extremely ingenious in making their webs, spiders are patient and industrious and so can stand for these qualities.

Web

The round web of the spider has been called the Wheel of Fate among Hindus. The Goddess is the spinner, sitting at the center of her wheel. The most wheel-like creation of the spider is that of the orb web spider, which is rounded with lines coming out from the center like spokes. Spiders' silk is a fibrous kind of protein. It is insoluble in water and is almost as strong as high-tensile nylon thread, although it is much more elastic. There are many varieties of spider, however, which use silk in different forms. Their food is mainly insects caught in the web, but some eat lizards or birds.

Among the Jicarilla Apaches, spider webs are equated with sunbeams. In birth rites, a cord of unblemished buckskin called "spider's rope" is stretched from the umbilicus of the newborn child towards the sun. Spider Girls help Monster-Slayer survive the cold by weaving cloth, which gives him sacred power for his journey to the sun. In a Navajo legend, Spider Woman and Spider Man exhale webs to hold back the waters during the time of emergence.

The Navajos saw spinning and weaving in terms of their relationship with the sheep and the yarn. Interaction with the raw materials enacts myth and religious belief. Spider Woman's weaving can relate to the healing of individuals. By spinning the yarn sunwise, unraveling is prevented. This would, in the metaphoric sense, stop any threat to health and cosmic harmony. The spider's web is often symbolic of weaving and textiles. There was a commercial rivalry between Athena's city of Athens and the seamen of Crete. Many seals with the emblem of a spider were found at Miletus, Crete.

In Greek myth, after Athena turned Arachne into a spider, Arachne saved herself by climbing up her web. The fly was thought to be the embodiment of the human soul passing from one life to the next. Since the spider was a totem of Athena, weaver of Fate, man's helplessness in the web of Fate was symbolized by the fly in a spider's web.

Exploring Your Cronehood:
The Crone Journal

—J.R.

Years of living have demonstrated that sometimes things do not go exactly as we would like them to: The cable guy hooks up your cable to your electric alarm clock instead of your TV, your dentist insults both your looks and your intelligence by suggesting unnecessary and expensive cosmetic dental work, and a friend turns something you said upside down, and now you have to deal with the backlash. What's a Crone to do? The primary response is that a Crone needs to be more authentically herself.

- She finds ways to express her needs and concerns while avoiding chaos.
- She strives to create a world that includes friends who are truthful.
- She maintains her compassion even at times when her soul urges her to speak out in strength.

I will not stand at the feet of hyenas and say nothing.
Though scavengers have their place
And bring into the world their particular wild sound,
I will not tolerate them at my door.
I am tired of loud bleating, of hard egos competing
And running amuck to reach the top,
I prefer solitude.

*I would rather watch waves turn away from the prow of a
   boat
In beautiful undulating rhythms.
I would rather nurture a rose until soft petals open with
   fragrance.
I would rather have the honor of stroking the fur of an
   untamed feline.
You know, there is more than one kind of success.*

*I will not be Cinderella, awaiting the Prince.
Nor will I wait dressed in jewels for a handsome pauper.
I will do my own laundry, but I will not scrub your floor,
Unless you are in true need.
I will not bow to a master and work until midnight.
Nor will I work in dark, musty, cramped quarters.
I will not allow my personal territory to be searched,
Nor will I be deceived by lying, smiling voices.
Spiders in the bathroom would be much more interesting
   than that.*

*I will not perform or dance as you think I should;
I will be who I am.
I will not lie about what I feel; it's too much work.
I will not open the door to false friendship;
Unless of course, I am sending it away to a more suitable
   partner.*

*I will not tip the waiter who spills a drink on my lap,
Nor will I remain on the table of a sadistic masseuse.
Once I accept the "I will nots" into the light of my soul.
We become Lovers, and I am at peace.*

Setting boundaries can be an ongoing challenge. Some may be surprised at our outspoken words, but speaking out is honest and is the only way to communicate what you don't want. As we move into our later years we are supported by our past experiences. A point is reached where we just know that we have to live more honestly. Of course we are still learning, but we have found some portion of inner strength through some of life's hardships.

Human beings have the responsibility to make their survival choices from wisdom and compassion. It becomes our duty to teach others about compassionate survival. This is an ongoing learning process for us all, choices can be hard and wisdom is an evolving quality.

We are lucky. As Pagan women, we have the good fortune to see the Goddess all around us. We become pleasantly lost in the windy rhythm of leaves dancing in the boughs of a tree. We can see the Goddess Eos, the dawn, in the sunrise, or the Goddess Nuit, in the canopy of starry nighttime. In every time and place on earth and in the heavens, her essence feeds our soul. To view life through this kind of sacred appreciation is another aspect of the Crone's knowledge.

In this chapter you will be guided to explore yourself and to create a Crone Journal. Your journal can become a place for you to explore your goals, praise yourself, and review your strengths and weaknesses, and it can help you make choices about your health. It is a workshop on *you*—past, present, and future. Your journal can be your companion, one that allows you a place for personal exploration.

Creating Your Journal

Purchase a blank book. There are many on the market in gift shops and in bookstores. Some are clothbound and some are leatherbound. Whether you chose one that is plain black or one that is highly decorated and colorful, make it something you treasure.

The Title Page

Create a title page. You might want to use: "Crone Journal," "Crone Book," or "A Crone's Journey." An alternate idea is to title your journal after a symbol, such as: "Crone's Cauldron," "The Raven's Thoughts," or "A Crone's Web," or maybe "Journal of a Wild Crone" or "A Crone's Musings." Anything goes. You might also want to add a Goddess name to the title. Write, draw, or paint your title onto the first page of your book. Signing your name is optional; some might want to keep their birth name out of the process. Some might want to add their magical name, if they have already chosen one.

The Dedication

On the next page, write a blessing or a dedication. Make this something that will shape the feeling of your work and inspire you. One example of a blessing is:

> *Mother of Life, Death, and Rebirth,*
> *Make this a true Book of Magic.*
> *Send through these pages a great light and power*
> *To renew and bless, to heal and to create love.*
> *So be it.*

Table of Contents

On the following page, write the table of contents. The finishing touch, when you have completed the journal, is to number each page, and then add the page number for each table-of-contents entry. Following is a sample table of contents you might want to adapt. Or, don't write in a table of contents yet. Let your journal become a more freeform way of expression. You can save the page and write the contents in when you've completed the book.

Sample Table of Contents

1. Praising My Wisdom
2. Acknowledging My Talents
3. My Follies
4. Exploring My Goals
5. Becoming Hale and Healthy
6. Loving the World and Being of Service

Your journal is almost ready to begin to use. One more thing you can do is bless your journal. The following is a suggested ceremony. Feel free to adapt and change it according to your need.

Journal Blessing Ceremony

The purpose of this ceremony is to bless and sanctify your journal. On your altar, place four candles at the four directions. Do not light the candles until after the ceremony. For the element air, place feathers or drawings of feathers, an incense burner, and a white candle in the east. For the element fire, use a red candle with red flower petals around it in the south. For the element water, place seashells and a cup of water next to a blue candle in the west. Place a scented oil of your choice in the west, also. For the element earth, place a ring of grain around a green candle in the north. Decorate this with leaves and a few flowers. For incense, try a resin such as frankincense, myrrh, liquid amber, or copal. These are used on a lit censer coal. Light the coal, place the resin on the coal, and begin.

Chant: *Omm . . . maah . . .*
Say: *Great Mother, I call to You.*
Bring to this rite Your love and
The blessings of all of Your sacred elements.
Come and bless this book and make it holy.
May magic and miracles rise from its pages,
And create the blessings of a lifetime.
So be it.

Pick up the book and pass it over the smoke saying:

Sweet and fragrant smoke, bless these pages,
As the powers of air sanctify this book.
Within shall be a path to truth and wisdom.
So be it.

Pass the book quickly over the red candle saying:

Holy light sanctify this book,
And may the powers of fire shine through it
With passion and love.
So be it.

Pass the book over the cup of water. Anoint the spine of the book with a little scented oil saying:

> *May purity bless this book*
> *And may the powers of water sanctify it*
> *With a new vision and a fresh beginning,*
> *To awaken those things that are unfulfilled.*
> *So be it.*

Pass the book around the earth candle, over the grain and flowers, saying:

> *May strength and beauty bless this book*
> *With the enduring powers of the great earth.*
> *May its form and creation grant me joy.*
> *So be it.*

Place resin on the coal and say:

> *With wisdom and passion*
> *I create a new beginning.*
> *With the power of the Great Mother*
> *Shall I work magic and re-create myself.*
> *I envision that my work will bring blessings,*
> *Not only to myself,*
> *But to all those I come in contact with.*
> *And so it shall be.*

Raise the book high and say:

> *Mother of Life, Death, and Rebirth,*
> *Make this a true Book of Magic.*
> *Send through these pages a great light and power*
> *To renew and bless, to heal and to create love.*
> *So be it.*

Wrap your book in cloth or tissue paper. Set it under your altar. On the top of it sprinkle a few leaves, flowers, and petals from your altar decorations. Let it rest for three days. Then bring it out and begin to work with it.

Allow at least one week for each section. The work that you do for each will color the days that follow the work. The ideas in that section will be brought to your attention. Allow them to play out a little over a week's time.

Choose a quiet, solitary time to do your journal writing. Create comfort: Light a candle and have a drink nearby. Put on some soft, gentle music. Do your writing in a notebook or on any paper at hand. When you have explored this aspect of yourself as fully as you can, then transfer your writing to your journal.

Section I: Praising My Wisdom

For the first section of your journal, consider your wisdom and knowledge. Take an evening to write about it. What wisdom have you gained in life? What knowledge and understanding do you possess that you want to share with others? Is there something that you wish someone had told you when you were younger? How can you save others from frustrations or misunderstandings that you have experienced? How can you help them make choices? What have you learned that has made living easier? Assess the wisdom you have acquired.

Section II: Acknowledging My Talents

In the second section, you'll acknowledge your talents, which include all your gifts and abilities. Often the word *talent* is thought of as being limited to artistic ability, but it goes much further than that. Your talents include any beauty or blessings you add to the world. Qualities you bring into relationships. In your current profession, do you have any abilities that make you useful and valuable to your employer? Do you have skills that enhance where you live? Are you good at cooking or gardening? Are you good at organizing things? What are the things that you love to do? What are you good at?

There are many, many good things about you. This is a time to applaud and praise yourself. Do not feel that there should be more; do not feel that there should be less. Accept your talents as being a perfect part of you. Write them down without shame or embarrassment. This is one place that you can say how great you are!

Section III: My Follies

In the next section, you'll explore your follies. Generally speaking, a folly is an action that is unwise, foolish, or reckless. Here we use the word to describe not only our weaknesses but also choices we may have made that were unwise. The purpose of this section is to be introspective about our past—not to find guilt, but to increase our knowledge. It is with the knowledge of our own inadequacies that we can find understanding and compassion for others. No one is perfect; but that doesn't mean we should suddenly choose to allow anyone to enter our lives. It simply means that we can choose to be more understanding of others. If we *can* forgive and understand ourselves, we can do the same for others. Still, as we can forgive and understand others, we must continue to do what is necessary to remain safe and protected.

Another reason it's essential to review your follies is that hiding them requires an enormous amount of energy. When we confront our weaknesses and learn to accept them, our energies become freed up and changes can be made. This section is about acceptance but also about the potential for change. We will have some limitations because of our basic nature. There are elements of our personality that are such a large part of who we are that we may not be able to change them. But we need to accept them all the same.

If possible, go out into nature for this self-exploration. Or create a situation where you will not be interrupted by family or friends. This section takes honesty and a willingness to see yourself in an objective way. Not being at home or around people you know can distance you and help you be less subjective.

Do your initial writing in a notebook. Then identify those things you need to accept and those you want to change. You may experience many emotions during this section. Let your feelings flow. Do not fear them. Performing this exercise will free you to concentrate on the next section.

Section IV: Exploring My Goals

Now that you've aired all your personal dirty laundry with yourself, it's time to take the next step. Crone wisdom includes the pursuit of your dreams. Limits on you are no longer what they were. You have the opportunity to reinvent yourself if you wish. At this point in your life, time has become more precious. We cannot waste it.

The elder years are a time to increase our awareness of things that bring us joy. Conscious awareness about our Wise Blood lends power to our magic. Believe, and you can achieve many things. In our quiet moments, we can enjoy the silence, feel the Goddess humming and pulsing within us, and smile at the beauty of the world. We regenerate and contemplate the many gifts that we have been given.

What are the things that you want to accomplish? What has been holding you back? Which things are possibly unrealistic? What things need time and patience in order to manifest? Find a comfortable, solitary place to do your writing. Bring along a candle and something to drink. Write out your dreams and goals on notepaper. Hold nothing back. Dreaming and visioning are part of your power. Be free in your writing. Explore every corner.

Section V: Being Hale and Healthy

We want to enjoy the rest of our lives. Preventing health problems is important for the Crone. Good health gives us the freedom to pursue our dreams and our pleasures. Simple changes in our lifestyle can bring magnificent results. The body responds wonderfully to diet and exercise changes. Encourage yourself with that little bit of extra self-love and make changes. Lose weight, drink less coffee, and decrease your salt intake. Doing so means you won't stress your kidneys and liver by having to take medicine for high blood pressure. Many areas of your health are under your control.

Following is a ritual to praise your body. Perform it the night before you begin your lifestyle changes. Light a candle and sit before your altar. As you say each line, touch the part of your body that the line refers to.

Ritual to Honor the Body

Blessed are these feet, which have walked the paths of life.

Blessed are these hands, which give the power of touch and creation.

Blessed is this heart, through which Her loving and living blood move through me.

Blessed is my mouth, through which I experience the gift of language.

Blessed are my eyes, which grant me vision that I may see this world.

Blessed is my mind, which knows and perceives things both earthly and spiritual.

Blessed is the whole of my body, through which I am able to journey through this world.

All honor to this body, and great praises to the Mother of Life.

Go forward and bless your body with the changes you need to make. Soon you will find great pleasure in this, as well as a sense of pride. When you succeed, others will ask you what you have done. Share the wealth.

Your Heart

Our arteries carry blood throughout our bodies. We need to give our blood free passage wherever it needs to go. If it is impeded, parts of our body can become severely damaged—not just our heart (heart attack) but also our brain (stroke). One of the things we can do to prevent this is to be on a low cholesterol diet. Without going into the percentages and ratios required for the "good" and "bad" cholesterol, here are a few simple things we can do to keep our arteries unclogged.

Use fats in limited amounts. The best choices for oils, in descending order, are: canola, safflower, and olive. Olive oil does contain more saturated fat than the others, so use it sparingly. Saturated fat is changed into cholesterol by the body. Products that are touted as having "no cholesterol" but list large percentages of saturated fats don't do you any good. Any fat that hardens when put into the refrigerator (olive oil, coconut oil, butter) has a significant amount of saturated fat in it. Avocados are also high in saturated fat. Remove skin on chicken. Increase the amount of fruits and vegetables in your diet. Include fish in your diet every week (fish has beneficial oils).

Exercise at least four times a week (to a limited extent, exercise can decrease the negative effects of high cholesterol). A brisk walk for thirty minutes, four times a week will help. Aerobic exercise is good, but pounding your knees with running can damage your body after many years, particularly if you carry excess weight. If you have ankle or knee problems, a stationary bike is a good solution. Low-impact exercise videos might also help.

Your Eyes
Yearly check-ups with an optometrist or ophthalmologist are a good idea. Any eye disease can be detected and most can be dealt with before they become problematic. For macular degeneration, a disorder in which the peripheral vision recedes to eventual blindness, there are several preventive measures to take. Wear UV-protected sunglasses when you go out in the sun. Studies have shown that dark green leafy vegetables, such as spinach and kale, and the addition of zinc to the daily diet can prevent or slow this disease.

Your Bones
Bone density loss (osteoporosis) can develop even when there is no evidence of this condition. There are medications on the market that can bring bone density back, but they have side effects. Prevention is better. To prevent bone density loss, exercise with small weights (that increase muscle mass and pull on your bones). Particularly after menopause, you need to get enough calcium, magnesium, and vitamin D. Good sources of calcium include milk products, fish, leafy green vegetables, and vegetables such as celery and broccoli. You can purchase a calcium, magnesium, vitamin D supplement. Magnesium is needed to activate the bone enzyme alkaline phosphatase. Vitamin D helps your body utilize the calcium.

One cause for osteoporosis is consuming excessive protein. Calcium is required to metabolize protein. If we are on a high-protein diet and don't get enough calcium, then calcium will be leeched from our bones. Areas of the world where people tend to have high-fiber, low-protein diets, such as Africa and Asia, do not see as much osteoporosis as the West.

Your Skin
There are at least a million skin-care products on the market. Here's an easy tip, borrowed from the ancient Greeks: Slather your whole body with olive oil. Go into a warm shower and scrub your skin with a sponge. Rinse off. Change the water to cool or cold water. Rinse again. Pat your skin dry. You will be amazed at the results. Don't forget to wash the bottom of the tub. It will be a bit slippery until you clean it. If you don't have time for the whole body, you can do your face, neck, and hands. After you come out of the shower your regular hand and face cream can be applied.

Aside from external applications to your skin, drinking plenty of water every day is beneficial for the skin. Becoming dehydrated can cause scaly skin and poor skin turgor. Carry water with you and drink whenever you are thirsty (even if you are busy). Also, smoking, broiling yourself like a lobster in the sun, and drinking excessive amounts of alcohol can have negative effects on the skin.

Caffeine or No Caffeine?
Now we have entered some seriously challenging territory. Caffeine in moderation (black tea, coffee, chocolate, and certain sodas) actually does have a few good effects for certain people. It is a diuretic, and this might be good news for those who retain fluids (although it would be preferable to decrease salt intake rather than use caffeine to address this). Caffeine decreases the diameter of the small peripheral blood vessels, and because of this it is a part of some headache remedies. It is also a bronchodilator, so those who have conditions that affect their lungs are sometimes mildly benefited by the effects of caffeine.

Now for the other news. Those women who have, or are prone

to have, cystic breasts need to omit caffeine from their diet. Do not substitute decaffeinated products, however, because there is still a small percentage of caffeine in decaffeinated drinks. Caffeine also contains uric acid, which contributes to the arthritic condition known as gout. It also stimulates the heart and raises blood pressure. If you have high blood pressure, coffee, certain teas, and carbonated beverages that contain caffeine are not advised.

If you choose to keep caffeine in your diet, try to switch to black tea, which has less caffeine with the added benefits of antioxidants. Due to its tannic acid, it also has an astringent quality. There are many herb teas on the market that have no caffeine at all. If you drink coffee and want to try tea, create a lovely morning tea ritual by using a special teapot and cup.

Your Immune System

There are many ways to boost your immune system. Vitamins and minerals will help. Get these by including lots of fruits and vegetables, whole grains, nuts and seeds, and milk products in your diet. If you have allergies to any of these foods, take supplements instead.

One simple thing that boosts your immune system is to get plenty of rest and exercise on a regular basis. We can't live our lives without some stress, but stress adversely affects the immune system, so we need ways to relieve it. Exercise is an excellent way to decrease stress. Entertainment and social diversions also work. Find ways to express anger or frustration that release these things in a constructive way, such as talking things through with someone or writing about them. Slow, deep breathing is also a stress reliever. Try taking several deep breaths at various times throughout your day.

Hormones or Nutritional Therapy?

Using hormones is controversial among menopausal and postmenopausal women. Modern medicine tends to treat menopause as an illness, when it is a normal process. Those who promote Hormone Replacement Therapy (HRT) play down the risks of endometrial and breast cancer. Scientific papers proclaim that when progesterone is given with estrogen, the negative statistics decline.

Even so, who wants to be a part of the percentage of a study (however small that percent) that shows that HRT can contribute to cancer? The amount of the risk is disputed and is not resolved at this time.

Difficulty during the transition to menopause can be caused by a nutritional deficiency, or by allergies. There is a lot we can do nutritionally for problems that have been described as "symptoms" of menopause. Megadoses of calcium are not helpful and can cause harm, but vitamin C, calcium, magnesium, and zinc to correct a nutritional deficiency can be added to the diet to strengthen bones. Women with diets high in soy experience fewer or no hot flashes. A decrease in sugars and the addition of yogurt to the diet can suppress a condition called systemic candida, caused by a yeast that lives in the bowel. This organism can grow out of control as a result of repeated use of antibiotics. Lack of energy, headaches, and dizziness can result. Eliminating caffeine and food allergen factors can keep energy higher during the day and improve sleep at night.

Exercise

Now is the time. If you want to continue to have a body that is strong and flexible, one that will serve you well over the decades of the rest of your life, you will need to institute a regular exercise program. There are many exercise videos on the market, from yoga to aerobics to low-impact exercise. Take classes, get a video, or join a gym. One fun way to exercise is to put on music and dance several times a week. If you already have an exercise program, write it into your journal and applaud yourself.

Whatever exercise program you choose, be sure not to overdo it.

Section VI: Loving the World and Being of Service

We have looked at our wisdom, talent, follies, goals, and health, placing our attention inward. In the last section of our journal, we place our attention outward. It is through positive ways of relating with the outer world that we keep in balance.

Some of the Mother's children are errant and unwise. Some of her children do not love themselves as much as they should. Some have fallen on hard times, have experienced ill luck, or were simply born into a place that causes them hardship. How can we help? Through our compassion for the world, and for all who live in it, we find the desire and the energy to take action and be of service. Balance out your self-study with service.

Find an area that interests you. Libraries need books, medical facilities need volunteers, stray animals need various kinds of assistance, local beaches and parks need cleaning up, people who doubt their ability to succeed need encouragement, people under stress need to hear a kind voice, women's shelters need donations, children without parents need direction and solace, hospitals need volunteers, neighbors need help when they are sick, worthy organizations need donations and letter writing, many environmental concerns need supporters. And so it goes. Acts of service will open your heart and the universal connections between you and all living things will be felt. Go out and bless the world with the love of the Great Mother.

Regarding Your Crone Wisdom

You have learned so much. When we taught the Crone class that this book is based on, it was wonderful just to sit with women and talk about what we had learned in life. Sharing our wisdoms was not only inspiring but fun. The Crone Zone ritual near the end of this book will provide a gathering where you can have this group experience.

Wisdom is part knowledge, part honesty, part justice, and part love. Life presents us with complex issues, not only about the world we live in, but about ourselves. Our Crone wisdom develops naturally through the years, but it gains an extra boost when we intentionally take a closer look at ourselves. We need to be aware of our strengths and form an appreciation of them. With honesty we can face our weaknesses, knowing that like others we are not perfect. It is in this knowledge that we become less judgmental of ourselves and others, and therefore more loving and compassionate. Our awareness of the weakness and follies in the world can bring forward anger, but it can also bring forward our love.

The ability to set reasonable boundaries is a part of Crone wisdom. Through our years of experience, we have become more certain about what we will not do. Somehow, we find greater ease in speaking out about what we believe in. Those of us who were, once upon a time, quiet and genteel little girls have found our voice.

7

Wise-Woman Crafts

In this chapter, we'll complete projects designed to celebrate the Crone, from creating a talisman to planting a herb garden to sewing a magical cloak, and more.

The Crone Talisman

A talisman is an object imbued with deep meaning and magical power. The owner sees it as possessing a certain idea or quality, or as representing a divine force. In *Arcana Mundi,* author George Luck explains that the word *talisman* may be an Arabic transliteration of the Greek word *telesma,* which means "initiation." We can become initiated, or blessed, with a divine magical force by wearing an object that carries that force. When we combine belief and imagination with the use of universal signs and symbols, we can create a powerful talisman. A Crone talisman is one that embodies the qualities that a Crone wants to bring into her life. It includes at least one Crone Goddess, one that is dark, wise, or magical, or at least one Crone totem animal. Several qualities can be designed on one talisman.

Figure 7a.

Creating Your Talisman

Ideally a talisman is made of metal, something that will endure (such as a piece of jewelry that uses certain symbols). However, you can also use wood, clay, or plasticine (artificial clay). The talisman can be round, diamond shaped, oval, square, or triangular. It will need to have a hole in it so you can hang it from a chain or a cord. The talisman design goes on the front; on the back, inscribe your birth name and birth date.

To bless your talisman, light a candle and ask your favorite Crone Goddess to fortify your talisman with the qualities that you have imaged there. Pass your talisman back and forth through the fragrant smoke. Visualize the smoke imbuing the piece with the energies that you desire. Wear your talisman when you perform spells or enact rituals.

Wood Talisman

Cut your talisman shape out of wood or masonite board. Drill a hole in it so you'll be able to hang it from a cord. Sand the edges, if you like, to give them a rounded appearance. Paint your design directly onto the wood and then shellac the whole piece. If you want a really fine line design, use a fine drawing pen to draw your design on paper. You can use parchmentlike paper for a soft look. When you finish your drawing, glue it to the surface. When it dries, shellac it.

Clay Talisman

Use low-fire earthenware clay. You can shape your talisman as you wish, including the hole for the cord. When it is leather-hard, carve designs in it with a wire loop tool. When the clay is completely dry, paint it with an underglaze (matte) in a contrasting color. Once you've applied the underglaze, wipe off the top of the piece with a wet cloth. The underglaze paint will remain inside the lines you carved and your design will appear. Another option is to use fine brushes and paint matte and/or glossy glaze designs onto the surface of your talisman.

Plasticine Talisman

Plasticine is an artificial clay that can be baked in a home oven. It is available in white, off white, or red-brick. Form your talisman shape and include a hole for the cord. Carve designs in the talisman as described above, or leave it flat for painting. Bake it according to package directions. After it is fired, paint it with fine brushes and acrylic paints. When your painting is dry, spray it with clear laquer or glaze specifically made to cover acrylic paints.

The Crone's Garden

Tending your own garden can bring great pleasure and satisfaction. You can use your own dried herbs and flowers in dream pillows, incenses, and sachets, and to make scented oils. Growing herbs and flowers brings you in closer contact with the powers of the earth. You will treasure your plantings as you learn about them through their cycles of growth.

Garden availability varies for everyone. You may not have the ideal space against the wall of a house or an apartment, but you can grow a lovely and useful garden in pots or a window box. Some areas have community gardens with individual plots available for local residents. Check for these with your chamber of commerce.

Place the tallest plants in the back, and those of decreasing size toward the front. Try placing a trellis at the back of your garden on which you could trail climbers such as honeysuckle or a climbing rose. Tall plants such as fennel look good at the back of the garden. Medium-size plants such as basil or carnation work well toward the middle. Smaller plants such as thyme, garlic, and dwarf lavender could be planted toward the front. Use chamomile, parsley, or thyme for the edges in the very front. Consider what plants have showy flowers, and intersperse them throughout. Consider the colors of the plants in your garden design. The dark green of rosemary looks great next to the gray leaves of lavender. Consider how a single color repeats in the garden, as well. For example, white: You might distribute white roses, white carnations, white feverfew, white chamomile through your garden; sprinkling white evenly throughout gives a pretty look.

Basil *(Ocimum labiatae)*
A summer annual herb, with leaves in varying shades of green and purple, one to two feet tall depending on variety. Basil is a basic cooking herb. It's good for garden borders and readily self seeds from its own flowers.

Magical Uses: (leaves) Love, attraction, prosperity, good luck.

Bergamot, Orange *(Mentha citrata)*
A perennial herb in the peppermint family, it has strong, broad two-inch-long fragrant leaves and grows to two feet. It has lavender flowers and can be used in tea, sachets, or potpourris. The leaves have a slight mint-orange taste that is nice for flavoring foods.

Magical Uses: (leaves) Prosperity, clarity of thought, success.

Carnation *(Dianthus caryophyllus)*

A flowering perennial, border carnations are twelve to fourteen inches high.Florist carnations reach four feet in height. Multiple strains have been developed in a variety of colors. They are appealing in border plantings. These flowers often have a rich, spicy fragrance.

Magical Uses: (flowers) Strength, healing, protection.

Catnip *(Nepeta cataria)*

A perennial spreading ground cover of the mint family, these plants have gray-green leaves, lavender or white flowers, and grow two to three feet high. They are self-seeding and attractive in the mixed border of a garden. A word of caution: If you have an outdoor cat, your catnip plant may be rather short lived.

Magical Uses: (leaves) Love, attraction, happiness.

Chamomile *(Chamaemelum nobile)*

An evergreen, chamomile is a soft-textured, spreading perennial that grows as a three-to-twelve-inch mat of fine aromatic leaves surrounding small daisy-like summer blooms. There are several varieties; the best one for making tea, which has a soothing quality, is of *Maticaria Retutita (M. Chamomilla)*.

Magical Uses: (flowers) Protection, purification, sleep.

Cyclamen *(Cyclamen primulaceae)*

A tuberous rooted perennial, cyclamen grows four to six inches high and bears white, pink, or red flowers. This one needs to be in a shade garden with indirect light. It makes a good decorative indoor plant near a window and grows well under trees, especially oaks.

Magical Uses: (flowers) Passion, fertility, happiness.

Dill *(Anethum graveolens)*

An annual herb that grows to three or four feet, dill is self-seeding and has soft, feathery leaves and umbrellalike clusters of small yellow flowers. The seeds and leaves have a cool, pungent flavor and are used in cooking, salads, and pickling.

Magical Uses: (leaves) Protection, (seeds) money.

Fennel *(Foeniculum vulgare)*
Fennel is a perennial herb that grows three to four feet high. It has yellow-green, finely cut leaves, flat clusters of yellow flowers, and is typically used as a seasoning. The leaves and seeds have a licorice taste; the stalk of the *finochio* variety is used for cooking.

Magical Uses: (leaves or seeds) Healing, purification, protection.

Feverfew *(Chrysanthemum parthenium)*
A compact, leafy perennial that will spread aggressively through the garden, feverfew has attractive, daisylike flowers and soft, fern-like leaves. It looks great planted next to roses, and tea made from the dried flowers is an old-fashioned remedy for headache. Its leaves have an odor that is offensive to some.

Magical Uses: (flowers) Strength, endurance, protection.

Garlic *(Allium sativum)*
A perennial bulb with multiple cloves, garlic is harvested when its green, leafy tops fall over. Garlic is a basic flavoring used around the world. Break up the bulb and use some cloves for cooking and save some for replanting. Garlic is also known to have some mild antibacterial qualities.

Magical Uses: (dried root) Protection, healing, banishing.

Honeysuckle *(Lonicera caprifoliaceae)*
Honeysuckle comes in multiple varieties, evergreen or deciduous, bush or vine. It has highly fragrant tubular white or pale yellow flowers and is popular with hummingbirds.

Magical Uses: (flowers) Psychic power, happiness, protection.

Jasmine (Jasminum)

There are many varieties of jasmine, both shrubs and vines. It has small, one-inch white flowers that are highly fragrant and can grow to thirty feet, but it is easily shaped to desired size by cutting back. Its flowers are used in perfumes; dried flowers can be added to tea.

Magical Uses: (flowers) Love, prosperity, prophecy.

Lavender (Lavandula)

There are many varieties of lavender, but English lavender is the classic variety for perfumes and sachets. It grows three to four feet high with gray narrow leaves and carries its flowers on tall spikes. A dwarf variety grows about eighteen inches high and has deep lavender-blue flowers. Lavender looks great in the garden planted next to rosemary and roses.

Magical Uses: (flowers) Love, purification, happiness, peace.

Marjoram (Origanum majorana)

Marjoram is a perennial herb that grows up to two feet with tiny oval gray-green leaves and spikes of white flowers. It's a popular seasoning herb, fresh or dried.

Magical Uses: (leaves) Health, love, protection.

Mint (Mentha labiatae)

Mint comes in many varieties and can be invasive in the garden, spreading from underground runners. It's best kept in a pot. Favorites are peppermint, which grows to three feet, with strong scented leaves and purple flowers on one-to-three-inch spikes, good for tea; and spearmint, which grows up to two feet with dark green leaves slightly smaller than those of peppermint. It has leafy spikes of purple flowers and is good on lamb, in cold drinks, or in apple jelly.

Magical Uses: (leaves) Money, protection, purification.

Mugwort, White *(Artemisia lactiflora)*

Mugwort is a tall and straight perennial that grows in a four-to-five-foot column with broad, dark green, sawtoothed leaves and late summer sprays of creamy white flowers. It is drought resistant and should not be heavily watered.

Magical Uses: (leaves) Psychic power, prophecy, strength.

Parsley *(Umbelliferae)*

This biennial herb can be used as an annual and as edging in an herb garden. It requires partial shade or full sun and grows six to twelve inches high with dark green tufted or finely cut leaves and is used for seasoning or garnishing. For best flavor use the flat-leaf Italian variety, which grows two to three feet tall.

Magical uses: Purification and protection.

Rose *(Rosaceae)*

A deciduous, bushy, or climbing shrub of varying heights and varieties, roses do well in both temperate and cold climates if correct varieties are chosen. The beautiful and fragrant flowers are used for garden decoration, for indoor floral displays, and, in eastern cultures, for culinary flavoring. Often used for perfumes and sachets, roses are highly attractive to bees and butterflies.

Magical Uses: Love, psychic power, healing, protection, good luck.

Rosemary *(Rosemarinus officinalis)*

An evergreen shrub that grows two to six feet high (can be cut back and shaped), rosemary has narrow aromatic leaves of glossy dark green with small clusters of lavender-blue flowers in winter and spring. The flowers attract birds and bees.

Magical Uses: Protection, love, heightened mental powers, purification, healing.

Rue *(Ruta graveolens)*

A perennial herb that grows two to three feet high, it has fragrant, fernlike blue-green leaves, greenish yellow flowers that end up as brown seed pods, and dried seed clusters that can be used in decorative wreaths. Rue has historically been used as a brush for sprinkling holy water.

Magical Uses: Healing, health, mental powers, protection, cleansing.

Saffron Crocus *(Iridaceae: Crocus sativum)*

These lilac-colored flowers rise in autumn from corms (bulbs). Crocus leaves are dark green and grasslike; its short stems are hidden underground and the plant grows three to six inches high. Saffron is harvested from the orange-red stigmas as soon as flowers open. Dry saffron and store in glass or plastic. As a spice, saffron is used in rice dishes of India and Spain. Use in the garden border; it's especially lovely among plants of low-growing thyme.

Magical Uses: (stamens of flowers) Love, passion, happiness, psychic powers.

Sage *(Salvia labiatae)*

Culinary or garden sage is a perennial herb that grows one and a half to two feet high, has narrow gray-green leaves and tall spikes of violet-blue flowers, and is drought resistant. Sage can be used as a seasoning in cooking, for tea, or dried over a hot coal as a fragrant, purifying incense (Native American use).

Magical Uses: Wisdom, protection, purification, healing, luck.

Thyme *(Thymus labiatae)*

Thyme leaves are heavily scented and somewhat drought tolerant. Lemon thyme was used by the ancient Greeks (dried over coals) as incense. Common thyme is a shrubby perennial herb six to twelve inches high with tiny lilac flowers. It is used in garden edges and is also a popular culinary herb.

Magical Uses: Healing, psychic powers, purification, sleep.

Vervain *(Verbena hortensis)*
Vervain is a short-lived perennial grown as an annual. It grows six to twelve inches high with fragrant, oblong bright-green or gray-green leaves, depending on the strain. The flowers are flat, compact clusters and can be white, pink, red, purple, or blue.

Magical Uses: (leaves) Love, purification, sleep, protection, peace

Violet *(Violaceae)*
Sweet Violet is the popular violet so loved for its fragrant purple flowers and dark green tufted heart-shaped leaves. The plant is eight to ten inches tall. Among the most popular strains are "Royal Elk" and "Royal Robe." Plants spread by runners outdoors or can be grown indoors in pots by a window. They require full sun only in cool summer areas.

Magical Uses: Love, luck, peace, healing.

Yarrow *(Achillea compositae)*
Yarrow is a perennial, free blooming in summer and fall. It has gray or green leaves with a bitter aroma. Flowers grow in flat clusters. Yarrow thrives in sun and is drought tolerant once established.

Magical Uses: Courage, psychic powers, purification.

The Crone's Coat of Arms

The Crone's coat of arms is like a shield or heraldic device. It is your personal emblem, which will bring out the qualities that inspire and empower you. Your coat of arms can also include a motto. It can be used on the Crone's cloak, or it can be drawn, painted, or framed as a picture, becoming an heirloom of your house.

There are traditional ways to describe heraldic colors: *argent* = silver or white; *or* = gold or yellow; *gules* = red; *azure* = blue; *sable* = black; *vert* = green; *purpure* = purple; *ermine* = white ground, spotted; *gutte* = covered with (usually white) drops.

The positions on a coat of arms, or shield, have specific names (see Figure 7b). When describing right or left sides, the shield is described as if you are wearing it rather than facing it. The shield is broken up into nine spaces: *fess point* = center; *center chief* = center top; *center base* = center bottom; *dexter flank* = center right; *dexter chief* = top right; *dexter base* = bottom right; *sinister flank* = center left; *sinister chief* = top left; and *sinister base* = bottom left. There are many styles of breaking up heraldic space, such as *quarterly*, *bendwise*, or *chevronny*.

On page 102 is a depiction of a Crone coat of arms. Its motto: "May Magic and Beauty Prevail" (see Figure 7c). This shield contains two crescent moons, stars, a rose, and two ravens. Using heraldic language, its description is party bendwise, saltire, bordered in or. In chief, above fess point, a sable raven facing sinister in a field of pale azure. At base, below fess point, a sable raven facing dexter in a field of pale azure. A new argent moon in a field of deep azure with argent stars, at both sinister and dexter flanks, each moon facing fess point. A rose at fess point.

There are many symbols that you can use on your coat of arms. For the Maiden aspect, you can use the bee, the bow and arrow, the budding blossom, all spring flowers, especially the lily, or the new moon. For the Mother, try fruit, the cornucopia, the chalice, the apple, the rose, the sheaf of grain, or the full moon. For the Crone, use the cauldron, spider, web, owl, raven, or dark moon. Review the Crone symbols in Chapter 5. Any of these symbols, in any combination, can be used on your herald.

Choose your symbols and decide how you want to break up the space of the shield. Draw your shield on paper with a pencil, using an art gum eraser to make corrections. When you have it just right, ink in the lines with a fine-point drawing pen. You might have your ink drawing copied onto matte cardstock, and then paint it in with acrylic paints. Include a motto at the bottom if you like. Frame it and keep it in your bedroom as an empowering image when you wake, or above your altar to inspire you in your magical work.

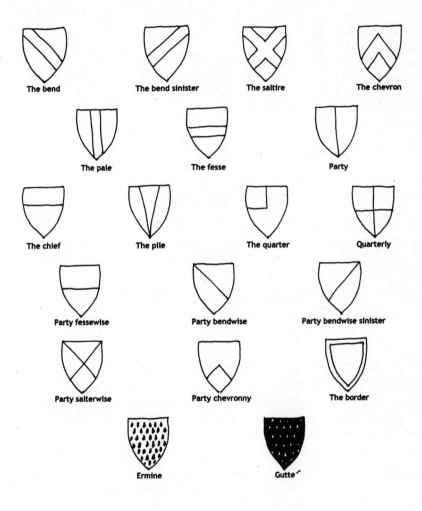

Figure 7b.

Figure 7c.

The Crone's Magical Cloak

The magical aspect of this cloak is using a cloth version of your coat of arms as a closure piece at the neckline. Choose a motto to go with it. This phrase, like a positive affirmation, will later be chanted over your cloak.

A cloak is actually very simple to make, but if you choose, you can purchase a black cloak ready-made and then personalize it by adding your Crone heraldic device.

The pattern provided here (Figure 7d) is one of a semicircle with a cut-out for the neckline. You can provide areas for the arms to come through the sides of the cloak, if you like. This cloak is best made with a soft black draping material such as a light wool, a thin corduroy, or a cotton-rayon blend.

Cut out the cloak as shown. It will be 40 inches long if you purchase 45-inch-wide fabric; 49 inches long if you purchase fabric that is 54 inches wide. Make pleats as needed to fit you comfortably around the neckline. Baste the pleats firmly in place. Turn the edges of the front vertical openings and the bottom hem under. Use black seam tape on the inside of the hem and the inside of the front vertical opening, and machine sew all.

Sew around twice about a half an inch from the edge of the neckline, then cover your sewing with black velvet or satin ribbon. Purchase 2-inch-wide ribbon. Fold it in half and baste it down so that half of it is on the inside and half on the outside of the neckline. Machine sew it down flat.

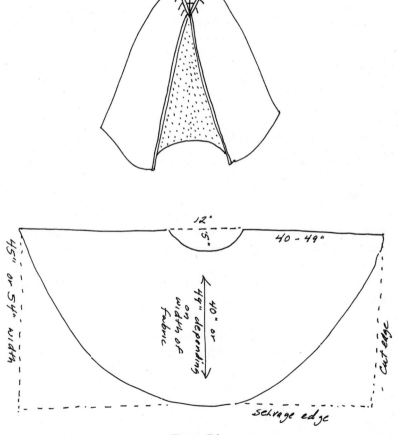

Figure 7d.

Cut the form of your herald out of a stiff fabric such as buckram (this is a material used to make belts and hats). Cover your buckram form with your choice of color for the fabric on the front of the herald. Later you will line the back of the herald with black fabric.

Draw your herald on paper. Decide whether you want to draw, paint, appliqué, or embroider your design onto your heraldic form. Transfer your drawing to your heraldic form by covering the back of your drawing with pencil and tracing over your drawing onto the heraldic form, as if you were making a carbon copy. Clean up excess pencil marks with an art gum eraser. Apply fabric paint, appliques, or embroidery. You might want to purchase a narrow trim in gold or silver to sew onto the edges of your herald.

When the front of the cloth coat of arms is complete, cover the back with fabric, turning the edges of the lining under to give the piece a finished look. Then sew one side of the herald to one side of the cloak at the neckline. Use hooks and eyes or Velcro as closures for the other side.

Magical Cloak Blessing Ceremony

When your cloak is finished, it's time to bless it in a ritual using your motto. Collect the following: an iron cauldron with fire burning in it (use one cup of 91 percent disinfectant alcohol as fuel) and some incense. Use a small brass or stainless steel bowl inside the cauldron to hold the alcohol. Place bricks below the cauldron. (You can use a stainless steel bowl alone if you don't have an iron cauldron.)

Place the cauldron or bowl in the center of the room. Open a window for ventilation. Circle the cauldron with incense saying:

> *Circle of smoke where thou art cast,*
> *No harm or adverse purpose pass,*
> *But in complete accord with me,*
> *For good I will it,*
> *So mote it be.*

Face the east: Call for the Powers of Air to bring magic and wisdom to your circle.

Face the south: Call for the Powers of Fire to bring passion and love to your circle.

Face the west: Call for the Powers of Water to bring beauty and deep feeling to your circle.

Face the north: Call for the Powers of Earth to bring strength and power to your circle.

Turn to your cauldron. Light it and say:

> *May the powers of earth rise to this place.*
>   (Visualize energy rising up as white light.)
> *May the powers of sky descend.*
>   (Visualize energy coming down from the sky as blue light.)

Call the energies up silently, within you. See and feel earth and sky energies swirling together within you. Pick up your cloak. Begin in the east and move through each direction clockwise: east, south, west, north. As you move through each direction, ask for the qualities of the four elements to bless your cloak. When you finish at the north, face the central fire and say:

> *Fire of deep earth and high spirit,*
> *Bless this cloak with bright energy and passion,*
> *So that as it is worn, it takes on the powers*
> *Of the chosen motto.*

At this point, stare at the flames and recite your motto. Then, move around the fire in a clockwise direction, holding your cloak and repeating your motto as a chant. After you have circled several times, put on your cloak. Stare into the flames. Say your motto aloud one more time with clear, focused, positive intention.

To release the quarters, move counterclockwise: north, west, south, and east, thanking and bidding the elements farewell. Now your Crone magical cloak is complete. Wear it at your next ritual.

The Crone's Incense Cupboard

Incense was used for sacred and magical purposes very early in human history. At least five thousand years ago, perfumed smoke was a part of ritual. Paintings from Babylon and ancient Crete show the use of incense. Ancient Egyptians burned it to the Sun God Ra, using special types for morning, noon, and evening. In Latin, the word perfume comes from *per*, meaning "through," and *fume*, meaning "smoke." A formula for manufacturing incense is given in the Bible. Today, frankincense is an integral part of services in the Catholic Church. The Chinese and Japanese use incense as a way of telling time, by how much incense has burned. Some people like to burn incense for meditation. It is also an excellent way to give a pleasing atmosphere to a special place.

The Crone maintains a well-stocked incense cupboard with ingredients and mixtures for various occasions. Our sense of smell can influence emotional states and can transport us to mystic vision or bring back lost memories. There are two kinds of incense: the kind that is self-burning, because it contains potassium nitrate (saltpeter), and the noncombustible variety, which usually requires burning charcoal.

It is best to use incense made of natural ingredients, such as woods and resins, gums, herbs, flowers, leaves, and roots. The ingredients are ground to a powder and mixed together to create scents for various uses. They may be purchased at stores, or specially made by the Crone with the desired materials, perhaps even herbs and flowers from her own garden. It is often useful to have both store-bought incense and the kind you mix yourself.

You can make incense to burn on self-lighting charcoal. It is necessary to take the ingredients you have chosen and grind each one to a powder, although a coarser grind may also be effective. You can use a mortar and pestle or an electric grinder for this. When the ingredients are prepared, the incense can be mixed. While you are doing this, it is important that you have your purpose for the incense in mind. This will impart a particular power to the scents that you are preparing. Incense should be kept in a tightly sealed container or it will lose power and scent when exposed to air.

A well-stocked incense cupboard might have the following ingredients in various forms for the right occasion: frankincense or myrrh, copal, rose petals, jasmine, patchouly, juniper, sandalwood, cedar, sage, bay, thyme, basil, rosemary, cinnamon, benzoin. A mortar and pestle are needed for powdering ingredients, although a grinder may also be used. A supply of self-burning charcoal and a heatproof surface to place it on are necessary for anything that is not self-burning, something like half of a seashell.

A round piece of foil about an inch and a half in diameter may be placed on top of the smoldering charcoal for better burning of the incense. Make a small cuplike depression in the foil before you place the incense on it. For stick or cone incense, use a regular censer or find some appropriate substitute. Besides being fire resistant, it should have a wide opening to allow for circulation of air. An apple makes an interesting holder for a stick of incense. Be sure to place a protective layer between your heat source and the altar.

Special types of incense may be made or bought for special occasions. Following are some varieties that might be of use for the Crone's cupboard. The amounts to use are not given, so you will have to experiment. In general, there should be more of the heavier scents like sandalwood, frankincense, myrrh, benzoin, or rose petals, and smaller amounts of highlights like rosemary, cinnamon, musk, patchouly, sage, or thyme.

Hecate Incense

cypress	*poppy or lotus*
musk	*myrrh*
patchouly	*mint*

This incense is to be burned at the time of the dark or waning moon. It is especially sacred to the Crone and evokes Cerridwen's cauldron of wisdom. Burn it to celebrate the ancient earth mysteries, the underworld, rebirth, and the realms of the subconscious. It is appropriate for creating magic and is associated with the crossroads and perhaps the baying of Hecate's hounds at midnight.

Full Moon Incense

jasmine   *sandalwood*
lotus   *mugwort*
benzoin

The full moon is a good time for rites of divination. Scrying, mirror readings, and all means of seeing into the future benefit from the full moon. It is also a propitious time to ask for the full emergence of something that is most desired, for this is when the strength of the moon is at its height. Mugwort is for clarity, jasmine is a fragrant night flower, lotus is for dreams and the pull of tides. Benzoin brings prosperity and increases divination powers.

Good Vibrations for the Home

frankincense   *sandalwood*
copal   *sage*
myrrh   *jasmine*

This incense is used for clearing a space of negative vibrations or feelings and for promoting clarity. It is also useful for protection. The scent sweetens the air and can be used for any purpose. To promote clarity and purity, keep a crystal in the container with your incense.

Love

rose   *musk*
sandalwood   *vervain*
cinnamon   *myrrh*
benzoin

Burn to promote the giving and receiving of love and to make it stronger. It can attract love and be used in a prayer to Venus/Aphrodite.

Protection Incense

frankincense	rosemary
sandalwood or cedar	*dittany*

This is useful for physical and for psychic protection, especially if you are doing divinatory work. Dittany is a banisher of evil and rosemary is burned for protection, healing, exorcism, and purification.

General Ritual Incense

frankincense	benzoin	rose petals or jasmine
myrrh	*sandalwood*	
rosemary	*cinnamon*	

This is a general-purpose incense which can be used for positive magical uses. It is also excellent for rituals.

Thurible Fire

Thurible fire can be used to create a dramatic effect of flames and smoke at a ritual and promote a scent throughout the room. It is also a safe way to utilize fire as long as you attend to the fire constantly.

You will need the following: a large, heat-resistant bowl, a wooden base to put it on, incense or scented oil, Epsom salts, 91 percent isopropyl alcohol, and matches. It is a good idea to have a towel ready in case of accident, but the flame is easily smothered.

In a bowl placed on a wooden base, mix a teaspoon of incense with half a teaspoon of Epsom salts and pour about three tablespoons of alcohol on top of it. Light the alcohol. The flames will flare up, burn rapidly for a few minutes, and then burn out. Be sure to watch the flames until they are extinguished. This is important for safety, and it will also empower the work of your ritual. When there is no more flame, the fragrance will remain and the atmosphere should be purified. Do not touch the bowl right away, as it will be extremely hot.

Making Your Dream Pillow

Getting to know yourself by getting in touch with your dreams gives you insight into your life and is an important aid to successful Cronehood. Now is the time when you can chart your own path. You are no longer likely to fall into traditional role models, which may cramp your style. Take advantage of this auspicious time, but first discover what really is going on in the depths of your being. You may have a few unanswered questions or ignored goals you now wish to pursue. There may be some part of you that needs healing before you move forward. Dreaming is a good way to confront these questions.

In ancient days, dream therapy was a method used to find a path to healing. The Goddess Temples of Malta had egg-shaped dream chambers where healing dreams were "incubated." A famous Neolithic sculpture of the Sleeping Lady from the Hypogeum in Malta shows the dreamer as she sleeps. At Epidauros, an ancient Greek city, rites of dreaming and healing were celebrated at the temple of the Healing God Asklepios. These rites may originally have taken place in caves. Sleeping in their depths was likened to sleeping in the Goddess's uterus before a spiritual rebirth.

To encourage dreaming, a dream pillow filled with potent herbs can help you in your nightly slumbers. For our dream pillow (see page 112) we will use mint, rose, mugwort, vervain, jasmine, and cloves. If you have any favorite herbs and flowers, create a mix of your own. The presence of these herbs and their stimulating scent can influence sleep.

Mint was used by ancient Greeks and Romans as a medicine and for its aroma. Peppermint can relieve headaches and other pains. When the oil is inhaled, it treats shock or nausea and improves concentration. The Roman writer Pliny said, "Just the smell of mint refreshes our spirits and gives zest to food." He recommends mint for stuffing cushions and points out its pervasive scent at country banquets.

The *rose* is the flower of ancient ancestry mentioned in many Greek and Roman writings. It was used for medicine, cooking, and decoration. Pliny, who had a strong interest in plants, speaks of the misuse of roses by the Romans, citing a case during the Second Punic War when the Senate ordered a Roman banker to be imprisoned for wearing a chaplet of roses in the daytime on his porch overlooking the Forum. The sweet-smelling rose is said to have rejuvenating qualities. It is associated with love and femininity and was identified most closely with the pleasures of Aphrodite and Venus.

Mugwort is known in Asian and European folklore. It was dedicated to the Goddess Artemis and to Diana. Made into cones or sticks, it is used as a heat treatment in Chinese moxibustion. By burning mugwort sticks close to the skin, acupuncture points on the body are activated. In various forms, it aids digestion, helps skin problems, and is an insect repellent.

Long ago, *vervain* was a sacred herb of purification, visions, and love potions. It is used in rituals to overcome fear, doubt, and anxiety. All parts of the plant may be utilized, but the pale pink flowers can be made into an infusion to cure depression, insomnia, headaches, jaundice, and stomach problems. It can be added to bath water to make dreams or wishes come true.

Jasmine is used in Asia to scent desserts or tea. In Thailand it is a symbol of respect, and garlands are used in Buddhist ceremonies. In India it is offered to Shiva and Ganesh. Often used as an essential oil in perfume, it is a relaxing antidepressant that can help tiredness as well as dry and sensitive skin.

Cloves were first used in China and are prized for their spicy flavor and highly aromatic scent.

Interpreting Dreams

Dreams are a kind of dialogue between our conscious and subconscious mind and contain many important insights. Everyone dreams, but frequently we do not give dreams enough importance in our lives, or know how to understand them. They fade away when we wake up and may be hard to remember, but the ideas in dreams can influence our lives and make clear our fears, hopes, and goals.

To understand dreams, you must remember them. Keep a

dream journal. Review your dreams as soon as you awaken and write them down in this special book or dream diary. Drawing pictures can be helpful, too.

Dreams can be encouraged and induced. That is why we use a dream pillow. It contains magical herbs that stimulate our dreams and make dream life rich and interesting. In a way, it is a message to our dreaming self that we are interested in finding out more about our universe. We can also send messages to ourselves before sleep that influence our dreams. Is there an issue that needs to be resolved? See what the dreamworld offers. Consciously ask for insight into a situation, a relationship, or creative problem. The mind continues to work, even in sleep, processing, storing, and finding the answers to problems that concern us in waking life.

Making the Dream Pillow

Your dream pillow should be made of a material you'll treasure. Silk or a fine cotton are good choices. Cushiony velvet is nice, particularly in cold weather. Keep in mind that you're going to sleep on your pillow, so first and foremost you want it to be comfortable.

Make your pillow a foot square, with a quarter-inch margin on the sides where you'll sew the ends together. Or, take a piece of material two feet and one half inch long and fold it over, sewing the open sides together. But be sure to leave open an area about four inches long, through which you can fill the pillow. Even if you used a sewing machine for the other steps, you should sew this opening closed by hand.

Fill your dream pillow with a half ounce to an ounce of the following: vervain, mugwort, mint, cloves, rose petals and jasmine. All these should be dried but fragrant. Fill the remainder of the pillow with batting, which you can find in your local crafts store.

Instead of creating a pillow, you might even adapt an old one, making sure the contents are clean and aired. When your pillow is ready, dedicate it with a ritual to bring you the kind of dreams that you need in your life. For an appropriate rite, consult our chapter on Crone Rituals for *Vervain, Mugwort, and Dreams* (see page 140). It can be used to activate the powers of your dream pillow.

Magical Mirror, crafted from a found wood frame, black acrylic paint, gold glitter, and red glass jewels.

The Magical Mirror

A magical mirror can be included as part of a ritual, or it can be an aid, like a crystal ball, for seeing events or to stimulate imagination. Looking in the mirror can be a magical act. You might be able to see the past, the present, or the future. When a Crone looks in the mirror, she notices changes in her appearance from her youth. Those lines and changes are something to celebrate. They show her good character, her sense of humor, her outlook on life. They are to be treasured. Beauty does not belong to youth alone. Beauty can grow deeper and richer with age.

Size is not that important for making your mirror. Find a mirror that suits your size preference, but be sure it is square or rectangular and framed so you can add a message to it. You may paint the invocation "I am Crone" on the top. On the right side, "Look upon me and"; on the bottom, "ponder my immortality." On the left side, "My soul will live forever." When you look into this mirror, you see not only your face but your essence, that which lives forever. It is reality and more than reality. This is what makes it magical.

To decorate your mirror, choose whatever materials you find appealing. You can try to make a mirror like the one we made, for which the most important tools were black ink, several good brushes, glue, and glitter. First draw the words in pencil on the frame. Be sure to leave enough room to center each phrase and space at the corners for special drawings. You may want to add Crone symbols at the corners—perhaps a raven at the top left, a snake at the top right, a cauldron at the bottom right, a sickle at the bottom left. Paint all of these and move on to embellishment.

Add a scattering of gold sprinkles around the inner frame. Pour glue where you want glitter to stick and scatter the glitter generously over the glue. Press it down and let it dry. Each of the outer corners is also decorated with gold glitter. Paint red strokes at the inner corners of the frame and add a red jewellike decoration on each side of the inner point of the frame. On the outer section, place a small red bead, like a Christmas tree ornament, in the middle of the gold glitter area on each side.

Bless the mirror with a ritual, then hang it in a place where you can see it and think about what it says.

8

Crone Spells, Rituals, and Meditations

You cannot have too many rites and spells in your lovely bag of magical possibilities. In this chapter, rituals, spells, and meditations will help bring some of your dreams into reality and get you to focus on what is important in your life, to honor the Crone, learn from your dreams, bless the world, celebrate life, and more.

Diamonds and Spiderwebs

A Spell to Manifest a Desire

Items Needed: Pieces of a spider's web caught onto a small stick. (Turn or rotate the stick as you collect the webs. This will be referred to as "the wand.") Also, morning dew gathered onto three leaves, a white candle, three pieces of quartz crystal (smooth tumbled crystal works well), a censer, myrrh resin, an incense coal, and matches.

The Altar: Build your altar in a place where morning light falls on the altar top. Place the candle in the center and the quartz crystals around the candle. Place the leaves with morning dew into a dish and set these at the right. Place the "wand" to the left.

Timing: Perform this spell at dawn at any lunar time between the first new crescent and the full moon.

The Ritual: Be seated at your altar. Place myrrh resin on the lit coal. Waft the fragrant smoke over your altar. Then say:

> *Spider, Spinner, Weaver of Fate,*
> *Catch for me the gifts of the morning.*
> *Take the drops of morning dew caught in thy web,*
> *And turn them into the riches of sparkling diamonds.*
> *Praises to the Lady Arachne.*

Pick up the leaves with morning dew, brush the wetness across your face, and say:

> *As precious drops of morning dew,*
> *Are the source of your diamond fire,*
> *So shall the fire of the young day*
> *Enter my soul.*
> *Magic enter, magic stay.*

Put down the leaves. Breathe in the young day. Let it fill you and awaken your magic. Say:

> *At each point of Arachne's web*
> *Does a drop of water appear,*
> *Shining like a translucent diamond.*
> *She catches the morning magic in her web,*
> *Just as I have brought it into my soul.*
> *Magic enter, magic stay.*

Light the candle. Pick up a quartz crystal and hold it before the candle flame. Look at the flame through the stone and say:

> *As I see her diamond fire, through this stone,*
> *So shall what I desire be held in my inner vision.*
> *What I see, is, and will be.*
> *Watch me, as I walk into the world and make magic.*
> *Magic enter, magic stay.*

Consider what you wish to make magic for. Set the stone down and envision your desire. See it. Hear it. Know that it is and that it will be. It is a possibility come to life. Pick up the wand. Imagine your vision before you, just floating above the candle flame. Point the wand into the vision and repeat the following three times.

> *Spider, Spinner, Weaver of Fate,*
> *Make true this vision, O Lady Great,*
> *Naught in this world, neither foul nor foe,*
> *Shall halt its power, or fiery glow.*
> *Hail to the power of Arachne!*
> *To catch a dream is to have it.*
> *Magic has entered and magic stays.*

Hold the wand in both hands and envision your desire again above the flame. Release your vision as you burn the spider webs on your wand over the candle. Say these words slowly as the webs burn:

> *And so it shall be!*

Triple Goddess Ritual

Celebrating Maiden, Mother, and Crone

Items Needed: Three candles in holders (one each of white, red, and black), white flowers in a vase, a red apple, a black cauldron or image of a raven, flowers for offerings, sandalwood stick incense and a censer, fine-tipped colored markers or colored pencils, a pen, and a journal or blank notebook.

The Altar: Set the candles, incense, apple, flowers, and cauldron or raven image on the altar. Have painting and writing items to the side, as well as the flowers for offerings.

Timing: Duration of this rite is one night, any time of the lunar cycle. It can be performed alone, or adapted for use by a group. It will bring forward the awareness of the Maiden, Mother, and Crone within you.

The Ritual: Cense the room with sandalwood stick incense. Cense the altar. Cense around your body three times by passing the stick behind you, hand to hand. Be seated at your altar. Chant:

> *Mother deepen within me,*
> *Make me strong and free,*

Then pray:

> *Great Mother,*
> *Triple Queen of the sacred and iridescent Moon,*
> *Joyful, powerful, and wise,*
> *You are the white dawn, the lily, and the crescent Moon,*
> *You are red as the blood of birth,*
> *As scarlet cherries, and as sweet wine.*
> *You are black as the cauldron, as the raven, and as the*
> *   deep night.*
>
> *Lady, deepen me in your Mysteries.*
> *Make my spirit strong and free,*
> *Deepen me in your Mysteries,*
> *Diana, Inanna, Hecate.*

Chant:

> *Black as her cauldron,*
> *Red as her blood,*
> *White as the dawn,*
> *I am she.*
> *Bound to her by blood and breath,*
> *She is Mistress of Life and Death.*
> *Black as her cauldron,*
> *Red as her blood,*
> *White as the Dawn,*
> *I am she.*

Light the white candle and say:

> *Sacred Maiden, I am as You,*
> *The dawn of strength,*
> *And the power of new beginnings.*

Light the red candle and say:

> *Sacred Mother, I am as You,*
> *The chalice of love and passion,*
> *And the overflowing bounty of life.*

Light the black candle and say:

> *Sacred Crone, I am as You,*
> *The deep understanding of endings,*
> *And the power of elder wisdom.*

Place flowers as an offering on the altar and say:

> *Flowers for the Maiden, the Mother, and the Crone.*
> *O Triple Goddess attend me,*
> *Come . . . bless me, teach me,*
> *And I shall listen.*

Pick up your journal and colored markers or pencils. On three separate pages, draw one or more symbols of the Maiden, the Mother, and the Crone. You can combine symbols into one design, or draw them separately. When you are done with your drawings, say:

> *Black as her cauldron,*
> *Red as her blood,*
> *White as the dawn,*
> *I am she.*

Go back to your journal. Review your image of the Maiden. Gaze into the candle flames. Now close your eyes and imagine the Maiden coming to you. Look at her closely. See her give you a gift and perhaps speak to you. Take as long as you need. When she is done, see her depart.

Gaze into the candle flames and say:

> *Red as her blood.*

Go to your journal. Review your image of the Mother. Close your eyes and imagine the Mother coming to you. See her. Allow this to happen in its own time. When she is done, see her depart. Gaze into your candle flames and say:

> *Black as her cauldron.*

Go to your journal. Review your image of the Crone. Close your eyes and imagine the Crone coming to you. See her. Let this take whatever time necessary. When she is done, see her depart. Write down the highlights of your inner journeys. Then face your altar and say:

> *Many thanks and much honor*
> *To the Triple Goddess,*
> *May the Maiden, Mother, and Crone*
> *Continue to teach,*
> *Bless, and protect me.*
> *And so it shall be.*

Bow your head to the Triple Goddess. Let the candles burn completely.

Persephone Spell

Transforming the Seemingly Impossible

Items Needed: A white candle plus one of another color that you choose to represent your adversary or negative situation; string, scissors, a black bowl, a chalice of water, paper, pen, incense coal, censer, frankincense, tongs, and Epsom salts.

The Altar: Place both your candles in holders in the center of the altar. Tie them together with the string, but leave a small space between them. Have the other items arranged on the altar as you will.

Timing: This ritual is best done during the waning moon or dark moon.

The Ritual: Light the censer coal five minutes ahead of the rite. When you are ready to begin, place a little frankincense resin on the coal. Raise the censer above you and lower it to the floor below you. Circle your body once with the smoking censer, saying:

> *For purity and sacred magic.*

Light the white candle and say:

> *This candle represents myself,*
> *This is* [say your name].

Then light the other candle and say:

> *This candle represents my adversary,*
> *This is* [describe your opponent].

Begin your invocation of Persephone. Place frankincense on the coal. Raise the smoking censer in the air, saying:

> *Hail Persephone!*

Set the censer down and say:

> *Goddess of the Underworld, you abide in Death's Domain,*
> *In the great Halls of Justice, within the realm of Tartarus.*

Your lot is to stand before those who cannot go to Elysium,
And dispense their fate, with your divine and rightful
*   hand.*

Persephone, you are wise, O Mistress of Justice and Fate.
You have taken those who are fierce and unkind,
Those who have wantonly caused pain to others,

And you transform them, a seemingly impossible task.
With your power you cause them to care and to feel for
*   others.*
Therefore do they know remorse, and change themselves
*   from within.*

O Dark Queen of Hades, whose power none can stop,
Within your heart rests the tender Maiden who knows of
*   fairer days.*
Come then, you who are both fair and wise, hear my
*   request.*
Come, and through you we shall create the magic of
*   transformation.*

Now tell Persephone what or who is troubling you by writing it all down on the paper. Let her receive what you say. See her place her hand on your heart. When you are ready, fold your paper. Set it down on the altar, then proceed.

Persephone, I place my love before you,
I am humbled by your crown of patience
And by the power of your scepter
With which you dispense sure and divine justice.

Therefore, I ask that you create justice for me,
And right this situation about which I have come.
As I set this paper on fire, may this trouble dissipate.
By its ashes, shall I know that it will be gone.

Burn the paper, holding it over the black bowl with the tongs. Let the ashes and burned paper fall into the bowl. Then pick up the scissors and say:

> *As I cut the cord that has tied me to this difficulty,*
> *So I cut away the negative powers*
> *Of the one who has been my adversary.*

Cut the string that ties the candles together. Burn the string over the black bowl. Set the black bowl aside. Put frankincense on the coal and allow it to waft over the two candles. Then pull the candles away from each other and say:

> *As I pull the candles away from each other,*
> *So does my former adversary lose any power to injure me.*
> *Within me is the power of Persephone. I act through her*
> *   power.*
> *The negative power is cut away from me.*

Put the candles on opposite sides of the altar. Next, bring the bowl of ashes before you. Pick up the chalice, or cup of water, and say:

> *This has Persephone gathered from the River Styx*
> *The greatest river in Hades.*
> *Within it is the power of endings.*
> *It will completely wash away this difficulty from my life.*

Raise the smoking censer and say:

> *Hail Persephone!*

Pour the water of your chalice on the ashes and say:

> *As water meets ash,*
> *So does the last of the negative power dissolve.*
> *As water meets ash,*
> *So are the last of the unwanted energies removed.*
> *As water meets ash,*
> *What troubled me is no more,*
> *Nor can it return to me.*

Lift the empty glass and say:

Hail Persephone!

Take the ash and water outside. Pour it on soil. Say:

Now shall ash be reborn as earth.

Return to the house. Cleanse the bowl with water. Say:

All is cleansed and made new,
And blessed by Persephone.
So mote it be.

Take the white candle to the bathroom. Take a warm bath in Epsom salts. Leave the white candle in the bathroom. Leave the other candle on the altar. Retire, and let the candles burn.

Dark Mother Meditation

Magic of the Deep Cavern

Items Needed: Writing tools and a candle.

The Altar: Your mind.

Timing and Instructions: Perform this meditation during the waning moon. It is suggested that you either tape this meditation to play during the ritual or have it read to you. You can do it with a group and a reader, or take turns with a friend, reading it to each other. Either way, take the usual steps to create a sustained quiet, so that you will have no interruptions. Have writing materials available so that you can write down your experience when you are done.

The Ritual: Light the candle and stare into the flame for a while. Then take a deep breath . . . and release . . . letting all the tension flow out of your body. Relax your shoulders . . . relax your jaw. You allow all your tension to ease away, and yet you will remain alert. This is a journey to the caverns of the Dark Mother.

Sometimes the moon wanes into darkness. The solemn crescent moves into the power of endings and dissolution. We call on the Dark Mother, Sacred Guide, and Weaver of the Web. O Mother of Night, within you is the wisdom of the world. We have come, seeking You, Seeking the Great Crone who wields the scythe of endings. All-Knowing One, come closer.

Dark One of the deep and ancient caverns, we honor you, knowing that all beginnings are rooted in endings. We will journey into your caverns to gain knowledge and strength, to learn to discern that in our lives which is truly important, and to learn to let other things fall away, into the darkness.

Just now, purples and blues move across your inner vision, and in the purple dusk, black ravens fly across the sky, piercing the night air with their cries. (pause) Her raven flies up before you, in magic and all-knowing, her eyes like polished black gems. You move onto her back (pause) and by the power of her feathers, you move through the purple dusk. Your raven is taking you to the Caverns of the Dark Mother.

Cool winds fly across your body. You are flying . . . flying upon the back of the raven. Stars gleam as you pass them by, flying through the night sky. (pause) You fly until the raven touches down. When you disembark, you find your feet on solid ground.

Before you, you see three cave openings. You choose . . . and plunge into a vast darkness. How large or how small the cavern is, you cannot tell. You keep to your left, touching your hand to the cave wall. You smell the air . . . musty, damp, and cool. Your right hand feels nothing but empty space. You continue on, hearing only the sounds of your own steps. And then a new sound comes to you, deep and rhythmic, and then singing, and a dark, steady pulse. (pause)

You continue to move forward until you come to a wall before you. Everything is pitch black. You feel the wall and realize that it is a gate. You push it and it opens forward. It is then that you become aware of another vast underground chamber. At the far end you see the warm amber glow of fire.

She is working with something in a large black cauldron, suspended over the fire, and she is singing. She must know that you are there, but she ignores you. You look behind her and realize that the cave is composed entirely of crystal. You come closer, listening to her sound. (pause) Yes, she is singing. Steam rises from the cauldron over which she works. Her hair streams up and away as if lifted by the vapors. You see her face. She is old, yet beautiful and ageless. Suddenly she looks straight into your eyes. She says your name (pause), and then she says:

> *So, you have come.*
> *Now you must learn which things in your life are of real*
>   *importance*
> *And which things you may let fall away.*
> *Your life is precious. Do not waste it.*
> *And when the end comes, let it come, after having lived*
>   *well.*

You suddenly realize that there is more to this cavern than you at first had seen. A great web, visible and yet invisible, fills the space, and she is at the center. She speaks again:

> *Come, enter your own deep darkness and we will look at*
>   *your life.*
> *Move downward, inside, to the inner depth.*
> *Move downward, dear one, into your own web.* (pause)
> *And now you are at the center of your own web.*
> *It is the center from which your life comes and goes.*
> *Look at your web. See the lines and the weaving.*
> *Those things that are of great importance to you, those*
>   *strands shine.*
> *Look at the shining strands . . . and tell me what they are.*

Allow a long pause, then continue . . .

> *Look at the lesser strands, look at these.*
> *How much of your life energy do you wish to spend on these*
>   *strands?*
> *Which ones can you release?* (long pause)
> *Now, release them.* (pause)

As you free those strands, the energy returns to your center.
(pause)

She speaks your name and says:

As you let the lesser strands go, you become more and more
free.
Let them go.
Let those of great importance remain, pure and sparking
with light. (pause)
When you are done, rise up and return to my cave. (pause
as long as needed)

Then you see her. She sings, and the air shivers and trembles.
The crystal cavern wall sparkles. The great web glistens, and you
know that the web within you glistens together with it. You are
alive and lit from within. You feel a new sense of freedom. You
hear a low humming sound that blends with the singing of the
Dark Mother. She speaks:

Farewell and remember what I have shown you.
Come again to me when you will. I am always here.
Farewell.

Her voice falls away. The low humming sounds continue. The
sounds move you back, back away from the cauldron, back, back
through the dark cavern until her fire is just an amber glow in the
distance. Your back touches a smooth, cool surface. It is the gate.
It swings open and lets you into the dark open space where you
first stood. You move forward, feeling the cave wall with your
right hand. The air is again cool, and musty.

You hear the beating of wings and now . . . you exit the cavern.
The raven is once again before you. You climb upon her back and
again fly through the purple sky. The raven's cry pierces the night
air. It is a cry of joy. Purples and blues move across your inner vision. You breathe in deeply.

You remember your visions and the strands of the web. You remember which things are of true importance. You breathe deeply. Now you move your hands and your feet . . . returning to your body in this time and place. You open your eyes and prepare to write down the memories of your visit to the Caverns of the Dark Mother. Her blessings are upon you. So be it.

Light Begets Light

A Group Ritual for World Healing

Items Needed: Sage incense, a white candle brought by each attendee, a vase of flowers containing a leafy green branch, and a paper for each participant that has the following written on it: *"We come together for one purpose, to bring healing to our world. In accord with 'As Above, So Below,' we must work this healing in our own lives. Therefore, we agree to release old grievances, to set reasonable boundaries, and to release prejudice. Loving, protected, and safe, these things are we. These things we promote. So shall it be."* Place these papers in a bowl or basket.

The Altar: Place the vase of flowers in the center of the altar. Place the white candles of the attendees around the edge. Put the bowl or basket of papers under the table. Have a chair for each participant or pillows on the floor around the altar.

Timing and Instructions: Gather your friends together during the waxing moon. All should bring food for a potluck feast.

The Ritual: First cense the room with sage. Then begin as the leader picks up the leafy green branch.

Leader

Great Mother of Mercy who has many names,
Kwan Yin, Tara, Isis, Mari, Sophia,
We have great need of your loving heart.
Come and attend this holy rite,
We wish to help bring your light and power into our world,
To help heal this place of any grief and sorrow.

Help us to release prejudice and hatred.
We believe in your miracles,
O compassionate and loving Mother.
Help us to bless all.

The leader passes the green branch to another participant, who then invokes her most beloved form of the Goddess to bless the rite. The branch is passed around the circle and each participant gets a chance to call upon the form of the Goddess they love. At the end, the branch is put back into the vase of flowers.

Leader (*statement of purpose*)

We come together for one purpose,
To bring healing to the people of earth.
To release old grievances,
To help provide for others,
To set reasonable boundaries,
And to release all prejudice.
In accord with "As Above, So Below,"
We must work this healing in our own lives,
By the power of the Great Mother.

Leader hands out the papers in the basket (or bowl).

All Participants (*Reading together from the paper*)

We come together for one purpose,
To bring healing to the people of earth.
In accord with "As Above, So Below,"
We must work this healing in our own lives.

Therefore, we agree:
To release old grievances,
To release prejudice,
And to set reasonable boundaries.

One by one, these things we will become.
And so it shall be.

All *(chant three times)*

On wings we fly to magic high,
Raise the power of leafy bower,
Earth and stone, water and fire,
Bring to life our desire.

Leader guides all to raise energy

Stand and join hands in circle around the altar. Raise energy from
the earth. Close your eyes and envision that you are a tree. Your
roots reach deep into the earth. With your breath, draw up power
from deep below. Feel it flow out through your branches. Do this
several times. Then, with the breath, draw energy down through
your branches. Let it fill your body. Alternate, drawing up energy
through your roots, and then through your branches, always with
the breath. Let your energies flow clockwise around the circle
through your hands as white light. End by letting the light of the
circle rise up, flow below you, move out before you, and then
move out behind you. Then all say:

All

I am light, I am light, I am light.

Repeat the chant, this time walking clockwise in the circle as
you go.

On wings we fly to magic high,
Raise the power of leafy bower,
Earth and stone, water and fire,
Bring to life our desire.

Candle lighting

Each participant lights their candle beginning their statement with
their wish to heal the world. Begin their candle lighting with:

I bless this world with loving. . . .

End with:

> *By the power of the Great Mother.*

Leader

We send our light around the world.
The wisdom to heal old grievances comes to the minds of
* all.*
The desire to help others comes to the minds of all,
A feeling of open-heartedness and love comes to the hearts
* of all.*
We see this is a silver-white light and we send it around
* the earth.*
Light begets light, and wisdom and love begin to flourish
* on earth.*
All visualize this silver-white light flowing around earth,
Into the minds and hearts of all.

Pause to allow the visualization. Participants can speak out and state the positive images they see in the silver-white light, flowing around the earth.

Leader

Light begets light, as it flows around the earth.

All repeat

Light begets light, as it flows around the earth.

Then bind the vision to your purpose. Repeat the following nine times, increasing in intensity as you go:

All

And now by the power of three times three,
As we will it, so shall it be!

At the last "so shall it be!" release the energy and the vision. Let it all go. Relax your body. Hang forward at the waist, or lay down on the floor. Let it all go and make your minds blank.

Leader

Many thanks to the Goddess
Who will carry our vision around the world.
Great Mother of Mercy who has many names,
Kwan Yin, Tara, Isis, Mari, Sophia,
We are thankful for your loving heart.
Thanks and praises to You.

Blessings to all. May the circle be open but unbroken,
Merry meet and merry part, and merry meet again!
Now to the feast!

Hecate's Crossroads Cafe

Through the ages, like a moon partly covered over by clouds, Hecate emerges with some of her aspects emphasized at one time, while others are perceived under different circumstances. She is a magician and transformer, a facilitator, and a healer. She is a Crone who has come into her power. Mysterious Hecate is the Goddess we associate with Samhain, the festival between the Fall Equinox and the Winter Solstice—for who better to walk between the worlds?

In meditating on Hecate, certain ideas emerge. You open a gate of immense energies when you play with her. She is a dark Goddess, do not forget that, yet she becomes light. She is an ethical Goddess like Themis, who represents law. You must be sure of your motivations when dealing with Hecate.

Most important, she is a helper. She helps to birth things into the world, and she assists in their leaving. She delights in creation because her name is energy. She is the whirling spokes of the wheel. She is the spiral. You go into her and come out transformed. If you wish to practice magic, you must open yourself to the powers and be a vessel for this creation, yet always you are a shaper, like one who shapes pottery. What is it that we wish to create in our life as

Hecate Triformis.

a Crone: our life's work, the culmination of our wisdom, the ability to aid Gaia, the Earth, to survive in these troubled times, the ability to assist those with less knowledge to take their place in the world, the joy of creative power, or something else? It is a time to manifest whatever seems important to each individual.

In honor of Hecate, we try our hand at magic, and so we have a ritual of magic for a Crone group. We get together to raise a little power at the Crossroads Cafe. Hecate's suppers at the crossroads were an ancient tradition. This Crossroads Cafe is not your ordinary coffee house. The brew we pass around can be coffee, cider, or anything else that gladdens the soul. Refreshments, of course, will be served, but to get to the Cafe one must come in on one of the three roads marked out on the floor by black streamers. At the center is an altar where we place our candles.

Items Needed: Black crepe paper—about 100 feet to make the three roads of the crossroads, each road being about three yards long; three colors of ribbon—dark red, black, and silver or gold, to make wreaths for participants—four feet of each color per person; black candles with holders; incense (in cinnamon, sandalwood, cypress, or patchouli; materials for thurible fire (see instructions in Chapter 7); plastic spiders, frogs, and dogs (Hecate's animal) for decoration; a Hecation statue; sage; torches; sign for food area reading "Crossroads Cafe"; refreshments of black food, including licorice candy, black olives, chocolate, chocolate cookies, even caviar; large bowl or basin for fire pit.

The Altar: The altar holding the fire pit is at the end of the central path at the place where the two other paths branch out to form a V shape. The three roads form a Y. A large bowl or basin at the center may be used as the fire pit. Place four tall black candles around the fire pit bowl in the four directions. The rest of the space is for the participants' smaller candles in holders. These can be red, black, or white. Hecate incense may be burned at the side of the altar. You may also place sage for purification there. Leave room for the statue.

Timing and Instructions: This ritual should be held at the dark, new or waning moon. As people enter, they place their unlit candles on the altar and are seated in chairs around the fire pit in the central area.

A lecture and explanation about Hecate and about the nature of the ritual is given by the main priestess to set the mood for the ritual. Use material from Introduction. It is pointed out that we will walk the path of our life and think about the choices we have made and those we want to make now.

The Ritual: Explain that on the path to the crossroads we will be wearing wreaths we have woven ourselves. Making them is a ritual of magic. There are three strands: red, black, and silver. As we weave them and knot them, we will think of what we want to do with our magic. There can be a guided meditation while this happens, or quiet music can be played. Think about the path you didn't take. Meditate on what you want to create for yourself now on the road you will traverse.

Take one strand each of red, black, and silver ribbon and knot one end together. Braid the ribbons to make a triple strand with ribbons flowing free at the other end. Place the braided ribbon on your head and knot it into a circular wreath.

A priestess enters and purifies the circle with sage, which she places on the altar. Another priestess calls the directions. The candles are lit and the invocation is given. Incense in the bowl is then lit.

The main priestess recites the following:

> *Welcome to the Crossroads Cafe*
> *Hecate, here, will show you the way.*
> *Find a table. Take a seat.*
> *There's a couple of cats with a Latin beat.*
> *A little drumming to raise the power,*
> *For any hour is the witching hour*
> *At the Crossroads Cafe.*

> *Welcome to the Crossroads Cafe*
> *Hecate's here to point the way.*
> *Just sip that drink. It's topped with cream*
> *And laced with a dash of very strong dream.*
> *Hear that woman with the long hair flying.*
> *She's reading a poem of living and dying.*
> *You can listen to the latest spell,*
> *Or if you wish just show and tell*
> *At the Crossroads Cafe.*

Everyone sings "Ancient Queen of Wisdom" or another appropriate Goddess song. Have someone bring a drum to help with the pacing. As the chant goes on, the women from the circle walk up the crossroads, choosing one road or the other at the branching. Then they go to the altar and light their candles. They speak their purpose aloud or to themselves. When everyone has lit a candle, release the directions and open the circle.

Refreshments are served while everyone sits around and discusses their ideas.

Perfumed Smoke

An Incense Ritual

This is a Crone ritual that uses incense to help us work on our psychic talents and speak our wisdom. It includes readings for the year. Some occasions on which incense is important include the Egyptian Lighting of the Fires Day, the Eleusinian Mysteries in September or Samhain, the Celtic Festival of the Dead on November 7.

Items Needed: A vision-causing incense, either made by you, or store-bought (ingredients may be sandalwood, cypress, black poppy-

Snake Goddess and Snake, made of low-fire earthenware clay underglazed with a terra-cotta stain. *(Snake Goddess statue by Jennifer Reif)*

seed, mugwort, cinnamon, mace, orange peel, frankincense, jasmine, lotus oil. For instance, to sharpen psychic powers, mix mugwort, black poppyseed, frankincense, orange peel, and lotus oil); two black and two white candles; Goddess statue of your choice; the image of a snake, which may be kept in a basket; small candles with holders in violet, rose, and pale yellow or orange; a bowl and accessories for thurible fire (see page 109); a set of twigs or sticks— three marked for prophetic Crones with a triangle, circle, and cross in a circle; cushions to sit on during meditation.

The Altar: Place the altar on the north side of the room. Put black candles on the north and south sides and white on the east and west. Place Goddess statue on the north. Beneath the Goddess statue, place the image of the snake. Incense burns in the south. In the center is a bowl on a piece of wood for the thurible fire. Individual candles may be placed around the outer part of the altar.

Timing and Instructions: This ritual dealing with mysteries of death and resurrection is best done on the dark or waxing moon. The ritual will be for a group whose members visualize separately and then together. However, it can be also done by a solitary visioner with a recorded version of the meditation.

The Ritual: Cast the circle when all are present. Let each person who casts one of the directions light a candle there. The priestess lights the visioning incense. As she lights it, she says:

> *As I light this incense,*
> *May it dance the dance of perfumed smoke*
> *And bring us visions that speak to our hearts and our*
>   *imaginations.*

Then the priestess gives the invocation:

> *Persephone, you who have the courage to go down into the*
>   *Underworld*
> *To aid those who have died and those who are reborn.*
> *Come to our visioning tonight*

So that we may divine our true paths.
Take off the veil from the mysteries of life and death
At this time of the darkening of the seasons,
So that we may rightly understand the way we must
    travel.

Oh beloved of the Mother Goddess,
Speak through us and tell us truths that we need to know
In order to follow our paths through the mists
Of what is to come and what has gone by.
Oh sweet Goddess, protector of flowers
And all things beautiful,
Help us to also walk the path of beauty.

Everyone should be seated for the Visioning Meditation:

You are in a dark wooded space. All around you are tall
trees and leafy bushes. You are walking slowly along a path,
which is taking you to a very sacred place. You come to a hill
with a rocky outcropping. There is a cleft in the rock. You move
a few branches aside and go inside. It is a hidden cave. It is
dark, but ahead you see some light. You move toward the light,
following a path in the cave. All around you is the glint of crys-
tal. There are stalactites and stalagmites growing in the cave
and some of them are crystalized. You want to look at them and
walk along some other paths, but you must move on. Soon you
come to a wide room with a high ceiling. There is a hole in the
ceiling far above. You can see a little bit of sky and light coming
through it. There are stones strewn around the room and clefts
in the wall that can be used for benches to sit on. In the center of
the eastern wall, about waist high, is another depression. Inside
it is a piece of stone that looks like a standing figure. If you look
where the face would be, you can see that it is quite beautiful. It
is the face of the Goddess carved into the cave by water and time.
Sit down upon a bench opposite this figure and look at it for
a while. She is trying to tell you something. What is she saying?
It is something important about your life. Thank her for her in-
sights, but continue to sit and watch. You will see something

happening like pictures on a movie screen, or you may hear
sounds and voices. Try to remember these things. After a while,
if you feel you have seen what you must see, get up and return
over the path you took. Walk slowly and come to the entrance of
the cave. Take the path through the forest and find that there
are other people walking through the forest, too. When you come
out to the place where you started, you may open your eyes. Be
conscious that you are in the room. Smell the incense, hear the
music. Put your hand on the earth to ground yourself and
bring yourself back from the vision.

Now, stand up and take your neighbor's hand. Form a circle
where you can discuss your experience. The discussions should be
for about eight people maximum. If there are more, divide into
groups. After everyone who wishes to do so has discussed her vision, it is time for the group to get a pronouncement for the year.
From the set of twigs have each person take one. The three Crones
who get the sticks marked with a triangle, circle, and cross in a circle will be the ones who give the pronouncement. They will be
given a deck of Tarot cards to shuffle and cut. Each Crone will pick
a card.

A bowl for thurible fire has been resting in the center of the circle. It is now lit.

The three Crones contemplate their cards as they watch the
flame. The others also think about their visions. The flame will rise
about six inches high and light the area. Feel a change in energy as
all that is not needed is burned away and the air is charged with
something positive. The transmutation of fire is working and it is
good to visualize those things you wish to happen as the sizzling
and crackling of the salts in the mixture absorb negative energies.
The fragrance of the perfume in the fire should become stronger.
Watch the fire until it goes out.

The three Crones will rise and go to the center of the circle.
The first Crone stands for the past. She looks at her card and tells
what she sees. The second stands for the present. She looks at her
card and tells what she sees. Then the third, the Crone of the future, reads her card. A scribe writes down these pronouncements
so they can be preserved for the group.

The Crones are thanked and go back to their places in the circle. A chant begins among the participants. *The Crone Chant* is a good choice for this ritual, but others may be used.

Crone Chant

Scadi
Hokmah
Urmya
Urd
Durga
Circe
Ceres
Cerridwen

Crones be with me.

Oya
Minerva
Themis
Hecate
Morrigan

At the right moment the directions are thanked and the circle is opened. It is now time for refreshments.

Vervain, Mugwort, and Dreams

This ritual can be used to induce healing sleep. It is also a good way to empower a dream pillow, which you have prepared to bring you wise dreams. The ritual may be used by individuals or it can be a group ceremony, with separate people taking the directions and the blessings.

Items Needed: A dream pillow to be empowered (see chapter on crafts), incense of sandlewood or sage, rose water, picture of Artemis or Diana.

The Altar: Burn incense on your altar and place the bowl of rose water there. Place the picture of Artemis or Diana behind the pillow at the center of the altar.

Timing and Instructions: This ritual is best done at the full moon, but never at the dark moon.

The Ritual: After censing the room with the incense, call in the four directions as you hold the incense burner:

> *Hail Goddesses of the East, sacred to air.*
> *Make your winds swirl around our pillow, clearing and*
> * purifying,*
> *Carrying sweet scents.*
>
> *Hail Goddesses of the South, sacred to fire.*
> *Bring your warmth and passion.*
> *Lead us on the path we must go to the fulfillment of our*
> * dreams.*
>
> *Hail Goddesses of the West, sacred to water.*
> *You who rule the fluid depths of our emotions.*
> *Let our true feelings come to us in our dreams.*
>
> *Hail Goddesses of the North, sacred to earth.*
> *Ground us in the truths and the underlying realities,*
> * pedestals of our lives.*
> *Be our guide in all things of nature and the essence of this*
> * planet.*
> *Blessed be.*

Now we can begin to ensure that the pillow with its herbs will carry our dreams to us.

> *Gaia, sacred Goddess of the earth, our home,*
> *Creator of the plants that bless our lives,*
> *Come and speak to us through the green mouths of*
> * growing things.*
> *For we, too, are part of you and wish to know our fates.*
> *Come, tell us stories through our dreams.*
> *Weave your magic over and around us,*

Stimulating our senses to understanding,
Through the spices of your wisdom.

Teach us truths with the wise essences of Vervain and
    Mugwort,
Healers and dreamers to our bodies and souls.
Beguile us with the heady presence of rose and jasmine,
So that our sleep is a wonderful bower of magic bliss.

Help us to understand the web of our dreams.
Help us to ask and answer questions.
Help us to know the adventures of our dreams tonight and
    always.

Stand and raise your arms to the sky.

Leaf and bark, stem and seed,
Come and fill our dreaming need.

Lower your arms to the earth.

Pillow filled with knowledge, go
To the land of dreams below.

Turn once clockwise with arms outstretched.

Essences be here tonight
Touch our dreams with knowledge bright.
May the trees gather nourishment into their rustling
    leaves,
May the flowers show their colors and trail their scent,
Blessed Be.

Close the circle by thanking the four directions. Drink a glass of clear water flavored with mint. Place your head upon the pillow and fall into blissful sleep.

The Crone Zone Group Ritual

The Fruit of Wisdom

The following ritual was composed by Jennifer Reif and Marline Haleff and was used in the ritual-workshop that they taught together in the winter of 2001 called "The Crone Zone." This event became the basis for this book.

Items needed: A cauldron, a liner for the cauldron that can contain liquid, a ladle, glasses (one for each participant), four candles in votive holders, pomegranates or red apples, sparkling water, red juice, red cherries, paper and pens, a bell, slow trance-like drumming tape, sandalwood, a bowl of salt, items to create a cave (several yards of black fabric draped over pillars or other furniture), a Crone mirror (we used a mirror whose frame is decorated with Crone symbols and the words, "I am Crone, Look upon me and ponder my mortality, my soul will live forever, I am Goddess.").

Altar I

The altar inside the cave has a table that supports the Crone mirror, and a seat in front of the table. There are candles before the mirror and many Crone symbols and items, such as Goddess statues, snakes, ravens, spiders, and so forth. Include glittery items like tumbled quartz crystal. You can even sprinkle a little silver glitter here and there on the altar table. It will reflect the light of the candles. Set the altar against a wall inside the "cave." Place black fabric over the entrance to the cave to draw aside, as a curtain. Place a bell on the floor next to the cave.

Altar II

Line the cauldron and set it on the table with a ladle. Surround the cauldron with glasses. Place candles for the four directions around the edges of the table. Under the table, place the bowl of cherries and the sparkling water and red juice in their respective pitchers. This altar is set in the center of the room. Participants will be circling around it.

Timing and Instructions: Perform this ritual just before or on the dark moon. You will need to assign the various parts of this ritual to the participants, and so a pre-planning meeting for the ritual is highly suggested. All bring food for the feast.

The Ritual: Before beginning, light stick incense and light the candles in the cave.

Opening Circle

Chant and add free sound vocalizations that harmonize, building energy with sound. Sound rises up and then quiets back to a hum before ending.

Purification

Pass stick of sandalwood around the circle.

Four Quarter Invocations

Light four candles around the cauldron saying:

For the East:

Hail powers of the East, powers of air,
Bring wisdom and clarity to our circle!

For the South:

Hail powers of the South, powers of fire,
Bring energy and passion to our circle!

For the West:

Hail powers of the West, powers of water,
Bring love and compassion to our circle!

For the North:

Hail powers of the North, powers of earth,
Bring strength and growth to our circle!

Between the Worlds

In that place between the wave and the seashore,
At birth and at death,
In that place between the mist and the river's edge,
As within this sacred circle,
Do we stand between the worlds.

Chant *(Leader has memorized this and all follow along. Repeat several times.)*

We are women of the Goddess most ancient,
We are women of the Goddess most high.
Bound to her by blood and breath,
She is Mistress of Life and Death.

Invocation of Hecate

Hecate, Goddess of the moon, of the crossroads,
And of the dark cavern of mysteries,
Help us to share our blessings of Crone Wisdom,
And through this, we will be renewed in
Self-confidence, self-appreciation, and great power.
Hail Hecate!

Invocation of Cerridwen

Cerridwen, Goddess of the cauldron and of magical
* transformations,*
Through you may we find freedom in facing the mortality
* of the body,*
In so doing will we overcome fear.
Then in spirit, may we know the mystery and magic of
* every moment.*
Hail Cerridwen!

Hecate's Blessing

Pick up the pitcher with the red juice and stand before the cauldron saying:

> *Through Hecate's cavern*
> *You will descend to the Underworld.*
> *In the Land of Death*
> *Are groves of pomegranate trees*
> *Whose fruit has many seeds and scarlet juice, like blood,*
> *The blood of life and death.*

As you say the last line, pour the red juice into the cauldron.

Cerridwen's Blessing

Pick up the pitcher with the sparkling water and stand before the cauldron saying:

> *From the past rise all things, and so death is not an end.*
> *Seeds grow in dark earth, the remnant of all that came*
> *   before.*
> *Fear not the end, for all of your riches:*
> *Your love, your talent, and your honor.*
> *All of these feed you now and will feed you in the life to*
> *   come.*
> *All of these are within Cerridwen's cauldron.*
> *Her power comes bubbling up from the springs of the*
> *   earth.*

As you say the last line, pour the sparkling water into the cauldron.

Into the Cavern

A leader has memorized this, and guides all to chant:

> *Hecate, Lady of Mysteries,*
> *Into your cavern, where darkness will take us,*
> *Into your cavern, where rebirth will bless us.*
> *Hecate, O He-cah-tay.*

Turn on drumming tape. It is explained to the women that the process of each woman going into the cave will soon begin. Paper and pens are handed out. Women are instructed to sit back and review their lives. They need to write down what they consider their wisdoms, the lessons they have garnered in their lives so far. Explain to them that during the time they are all writing, each will be asked to go into the cave. A leader says:

> *When you enter the cave,*
> *Read the words around the mirror.*
> *And see the Great Crone within you.*

The drumming music continues while the women write. One at a time, a leader takes a participant to the cave. Standing outside of the cave, the leader faces the participant. The participant and the leader place palms to palms while the following words are spoken by a leader:

> *Enter her cave.*
> *You who are both mortal and immortal.*
> *Look into her mirror and see her sacred signs.*
> *Honor your wisdom and your talents,*
> *And know your great power.*

A participant enters the cave. Two minutes or so are allotted. When the time has passed, the bell rings and the "cave curtain" is opened to signal the woman inside that it is time to come out.

A leader anoints the participant's forehead with water saying:

> *You have entered her cave*
> *And looked into the mirror of wisdom.*
> *You are Maiden, Mother, Crone, all.*
> *Blessed be.*

The woman is guided back to her seat. A leader takes the next woman to the cave, and so on.

After the Cavern
All stand in a circle around the cauldron. The following words are passed around the circle:

> *May the Crone's wisdom bless you.*

All Women Cauldron Blessing
Leader picks up the bowl of red cherries. She explains that each woman will add her own wisdom to the cauldron's contents. She demonstrates by stating her wisdom and adding it with the cherry to the contents of the cauldron. All the women add their wisdom and cherry to the liquid in the cauldron.

The Magical Drink
The leader places the ladle into the cauldron. She stirs the blessed liquid saying:

> *Stirring 'round this wisdom fair,*
> *By water, fire, earth, and air,*
> *To us this scarlet liquid sends*
> *The powers of Hecate and Cerridwen.*

Each woman is instructed to take a glass. One by one each ladles some of the liquid and a cherry into her glass. When all have a drink a leader says:

> *All say, "We drink of her power!"*

All say the words above, drink, and set their glasses down.

Closing Words
All circle the cauldron and join hands. A leader guides them by saying or chanting, or participants can repeat each line in echo style:

> *We are women of the Goddess most ancient,*
> *We are women of the Goddess most high.*

Bound to Her by blood and breath,
She is Mistress of Life and Death.

Close Quarters

Going from north to west, to south to East, thank and release each quarter and element. When done, all say the traditional closing words:

The circle is open but unbroken.
Merry meet and merry part and merry meet again!
To the feast!

9

Magical Seasonal Sabbats

As a Crone, you may or may not be familiar with these rites or with this type of ritual format. Others who are new to the craft may want to add this information to their Crone journal. Here you will find various parts of a Sabbat ritual explained. Simply put the parts together to create your personal Sabbat celebration: Build the altar, purify the circle, cast the directional quarters, invoke the deity(-ies), raise energy, include a poetic or mythic enactment of the season, perform your magic, affirm the magic, ground, perform the ceremony of bread and wine, close the quarters, and open the circle. This suggested pattern of ritual actions creates a very satisfying celebration of the Sabbat holidays.

I. Build the Altar

Clear the center of the room where you will circle. Place the altar table in the center of the room, or to the side against a wall. Set your altar with the colors, natural elements, and symbols of the Seasonal Sabbat. The altar includes a bowl of salt, a bowl of incense, and an incense burner. Place symbols of the four elements (earth, water, fire, air) in each direction.

For a center altar, place deity images in the center. For a side altar place deity images or icons in the center back of the altar.

Place images of the four elements as you will. You can set taper candles to the right and left of the deity images. Place all the smaller items needed for the ritual on the altar. The wand, used to invoke the quarters, can be leaned against the side of the altar table. Items for the magic section and personal cups for the bread and wine ceremony can be set under the altar, or on a side table. A wand is suggested to call in each quarter. This may be simply a tree branch that is held up, with one hand on each end, as the quarter is invoked.

II. Purify the Circle

Salt Purification
Circle the ritual area several times, sprinkling salt as you go, saying the words:

> *Circle of salt, where thou art cast,*
> *No harm nor adverse purpose pass,*
> *But in complete accord with me,*
> *For good I will it, so mote it be.*

Incense purification
Cense everyone in the group by passing fragrant smoke around them, or wafting it over them. Use frankincense, myrrh, or sandalwood, or another incense of your choice. Make sure to have proper ventilation in the room.

Sound Purification
All stand in the circle, and begin a humming *"mmm"* chant. The chant can be monotone, or done in levels of harmony. Voices may naturally begin to weave up and down. Later, this sound can form the background for the invocations.

Tree Exercise
Join hands in the circle. Imagine that you are trees. Send your roots deep into the earth. Let your branches rise high. Feel the power in

the earth, interlock your branches in a weaving, flowing Celtic design. Feel the connection to each other, and in the power of Earth.

III. Cast the Quarters

Each designated participant holds the wand and calls in her assigned quarter, to bring the powers of the elements into the circle. All face the direction being called in. Begin in the east and end in the north. If you are solitary, do them all. If you are two, alternate. If you are a group, then one person takes each quarter. The one who invokes the east takes up the wand.

Invocation of the East, Element Air

Powers of the East!
Raging winds and gentle breezes!
All feathered creatures
Who fly and soar on the wind!
Bring us your knowledge, your beauty,
And your keen-eyed vision!
Powers of the Air,
We call you to our circle now!

When you are done, pass the wand to the one who will invoke the next quarter. Say "Air to Fire" as you hand the wand to the south.

Invocation of the South, Element Fire

Powers of the South!
Great in beauty and enchantment
Are the bright Sun and the glittering stars!
Bring to us your power.
Swaying passions of love and ecstasy!
Like the center of Earth, whose heart is fire,
Rise within us.
Powers of the Fire, we call you to our circle now!

When you are done, pass the wand to the one who will invoke the next quarter. Say "Fire to Water" as you hand the wand to the west.

Invocation of the West, Element Water

Stand in the west quarter of the circle with your back to the center of the circle, and hold the wand upward.

> *Powers of the West!*
> *Great rivers and running silver streams!*
> *Deep oceans, and sparkling rains!*
> *Flowing feeling and bright courage!*
> *All creatures of river and sea,*
> *Who know the wisdom of deep waters,*
> *Bring your power and magic unto us,*
> *So that we may partake of deep mysteries.*
> *Powers of Water, we call you to our circle now!*

When you are done, pass the wand to the one who will invoke the next quarter. Say "Water to Earth" as you hand the wand to the north.

Invocation of the North, Element Earth

> *Powers of the North!*
> *Great Fruitful Mother! Deep caverns, and dark rich*
>   *Earth!*
> *Broad green forests and great mountains!*
> *Animals of Earth, bull, bison, and running deer,*
> *Great in majesty and strength,*
> *Bless our rite!*
> *Powers of Earth, we call you to our circle now!*

When you are done, pass the wand to the one in the east, who says "Earth to Air the circle is done!"

All say:

The circle is cast,
We meet as one,
The circle is cast,
The ritual has begun!

IV. Invoke the Goddess or the Goddess and God

You most probably have a favorite deity or deity pair. Here is a list of possibilities that will provide their own mythic-cultural influence, in style and flavor. You can focus on your favorite Goddess or use a God and Goddess pair. Have fun researching the deities you want to use. Here are some suggestions:

Diana and Faunus: Greek
Artemis and Pan: Roman
Diana and Pan: Greco-Roman
Woden and Freya: Saxon
Brigid and Herne: Celtic
Danu and Dagda: Celtic
Cernunnos and Epona: Gaulish Celt
Gwydion and Arianrod: Celtic Welsh
Ariadne and Dionysus: Greek
Cernunnos and Aradia: Gaul-Roman
Isis and Osiris: Egyptian
Inanna and Dumuzi: Sumerian
Ishtar and Tammuz: Mesopotamian

Write poetic invocations for your choice and then draw them into your circle.

V. Chant/Song/Circle Dance

This section is necessary in order to build energy. Use a chant or song. Here are three ideas; I encourage you to write several of these simple rhyming chants. Move clockwise around the circle, building energy, and increasing speed as you go.

I. Unto the dance, the circle cast,
Let the power rise and last!

II. Silver-bright, Full Moon light,
Heart and soul of Sabbat night!

III. Round and round the circle we,
Dance the magic brave and free!

VI. Mythic Enactment of the Season

Tell the story of the particular Seasonal Sabbat you are celebrating. You may want to add a reenactment, share some verse, perform a small rite, or create a symbolic action that provides an image or meaning of the Sabbat. See descriptions of the eight Sabbats, in this section.

The origins of the holidays presented here are Celtic with Saxon, Viking, and Roman-Pagan influences. The oldest Celtic holidays are the Major Sabbats of Imbolg, Beltane, Lughnasad, and Samhain. The Solstices and Equinoxes, the Minor Sabbats, were later additions.

Winter Solstice, December 20–23

From within her darkness I am born,
Lord of Light in fiery form.
Deep within her body Earth,
Leaf and branch now dream their birth.

Alternate Name: Yule, Modranect.

Primary Themes: Either (1) The Divine Mother gives birth to the infant Son, or (2) the Sun is reborn from her own darkness. The Sun emerges from the Womb of Night. Birth and rebirth, the tomb has become the womb.

Agricultural/Historical Themes: The agricultural field lies fallow. With the exception of evergreens, trees are bare. Natural vegetation has declined and is dormant. A time of living on stored foods. Winter Solstice was also known by the Saxon word Modranect, or

"Night of the Mother." The Goddess is the great dark womb of the long Winter night, ready to give birth to the infant Sun. She who slew the God at Samhain now gives birth to him at Winter Solstice; the tomb has become the womb.

The Norse word *Yule* was attributed to this holiday and honored the God Frey, a Solar King. In Gaul, the stag-horned God Cernunnos was celebrated in his aspect of fertility; the later named "Noel" log representing his phallic aspect. Ashes of the burned log were mixed with cows' fodder in order to help them conceive and bear successfully.

Celebration Ideas: Celebrate with a dance around a fire using this chant (either the first two lines, or all four lines):

> *From within her darkness, I am born,*
> *Lord (or Lady) in fiery form.*
> *Deep within her body Earth,*
> *Leaf and branch now dream their birth.*

Another idea is to create a wreath of pine, holly, and holly berries. Set the wreath flat on your altar and place white candles around it. Then turn out the lights. A Priestess or Priest lights one candle stating:

> *From the Womb of Night, the Sun is reborn.*

With this candle, the candles around the wreath are lit to symbolize the Winter Mother giving birth to the Sun.

Make separate statements about the myth of the season as each candle is lit. Have participants repeat each statement. Honor motherhood and the women in the group who have given birth, by inviting them into the center of a circle. Circle around them calling out:

> *Praises to the Mother of Life!*

Then call out Mother Goddess names to them such as:

> *Danu! Isis! Demeter! Inanna! Asherah!*

Another process might be for all to be seated in a circle. Pass a kiss to the one to your left and say:

> *For the Sacred Daughter of the Great Mother!*

or

> *For the Sacred Son of the Great Mother!*

Have each participant be birthed into a new phase of life, by emerging from under a dark veil to receiving a blessing. Priestess or Priest asks participants what blessing they require. Participant responds with one need. A lightweight black veil is placed over the participant, and the cleric says:

> *Safe within the Womb of Night.*

and then says:

> *Through the Winter Mother, you are reborn to . . .*
> *(affirm the blessing)*
> *And life begins anew.*

Cleric lifts the veil and says:

> *Blessed Be.*

A Priestess can appear as Lucina, the Scandinavian Winter Mother who brings light. She wears a crown of lit candles, and brings light into the dark time of the year. Have her hold branches of evergreen and holly, tied with long trailing red ribbons. She can make statements about illuminating the world with light, awareness, peace, blessings, etc.

Altar Decorations: Pine, pine cones, holly, and holly berries, oak, mistletoe, solar images against a dark background, gold, silver, green, blood-red, and white, image or images of Mother and Child. Candles to be lit for the birth of the Sun.

Imbolg: Brigid's Festival, February 2

> *Spirit of flame, of Brigid's fire,*
> *Work ye unto our desire.*
> *Dream with passion, fire in hand,*
> *Poet's heart, awake the land.*

Alternate Names: Imbolc, Oimelg, Candlemas

Primary Themes: The power of the Sun increases, the Earth's fertility awakes. The Earth begins to warm. Early Spring. Brigid, the Celtic Goddess of healing, poetry, and smithcraft is honored.

Agricultural/Historical Themes: The field is warming. Depending on the particular year, there is some melting of snows. Crocus and snowdrops bloom. Grasses begin to return. Imbolg is the traditional time to celebrate the Goddess Brigid. The light of her powers beckon Spring to be born. She is celebrated in her Triple aspect of poetry, healing, and smithcraft. Known to heal with both fire and water, her healing wells were famous and tended by her priestesses.

Celebration Ideas: To celebrate Brigid, you can heal with water or fire. Invoke Brigid and anoint participants with healing water from "Brigid's well." To heal with fire, surround participant with lit candles. Circle around the one being healed while drawing the energy of Brigid's fire up around her body.

> *Her sacred flame and her holy fire,*
> *Light of Brigid, light and power,*
> *Mother of flame and Queen of fire,*
> *Bring us Your light and Your healing power.*
> *Bring us Your light and Your healing power.*

Give each participant a chance for a fire healing. In honor of Brigid you can share poetry, or envision the power of her sword cutting through problems. Another possibility is to use the Scottish custom and place a grain dolly in a basket with a God image, to call forward the fertile powers of the Goddess and God of Spring.

Have three women stand in the center of the circle with their backs to the center. They can represent Brigid's three aspects of poetry, healing and smithcraft. Have them represent the powers of the bard (poetry), the healer (healing), and the protector (smithcraft). They can speak as Brigid, and remind us how these three qualities serve us all. To interact with participants, the three "Brigids" can dispense blessings to each.

Altar Decorations: A basin of water for healing blessings, tied scrolls of poetry to be unwrapped and read, candles for fire healings, examples of the metallurgist's art such as jewelry, chalices, or swords, many candles, silver, gold, pale blue, red, orange, and yellow. Images of the Goddess Brigid and of the young Sun God.

Spring Equinox, March 20–23

> *Mushrooms and fresh herbs to gather,*
> *Lilies and daffodils bloom*
> *Hail to springtime lovers,*
> *Sweep the circle with heather and broom.*

Alternate Name: Eostre

Primary Themes: (1) The Maiden of Spring grows in beauty and blesses the land. (2) The Sun Prince and the Maiden of Spring dance. As they court and love, life returns to Earth. Planting. The rebirth of plantlife, of new green growth and flowers.

Agricultural/Historical Themes: The initial planting season. Nature has become green and is beginning to flower. Spring Equinox is a time of great fertility, spring litters of rabbits and baskets of eggs have long been traditional symbols. Eostre (Easter?) is akin to the words *estrus* and *estrogen,* both having to do with mammalian ovulation. At Spring Equinox, the World Egg splits open and life pours forth. Nature experiences a great rebirth; the God is crowned with green leaves, the Goddess with flowers.

Celebration Ideas: Place several pots of soil around a central pot of flowering lilies. Chant to raise energy, and then plant the seeds in the pots of soil for new beginnings. Bless them with the powers of

Eostre. After you plant the seeds, a Priestess guides all to repeat the following lines:

> *Mother and Father of all growing things,*
> *Unto my being Your golden love bring.*
> *Bless this seed to fulfill its design,*
> *Of leaf, and fruit, of blossom and vine.*

Then each brings offerings of colored eggs and surrounds the pots with them. Place pots of flowering bulbs in the center of the circle, or on a center altar. Give each participant a cut-out golden Sun ray. Circle to celebrate the courting of the Lily Maiden of Spring and the growing power of the Sun. As you circle slowly, sing or chant:

> *Light seeks beauty, Sun seeks Lily Maid.*
> *Light seeks beauty, love golden!*

At the end of the dance place the Sun rays around the pots of flowering bulbs, creating a large Sun with flowers rising from the center. Feed each other berries. Light candles for new beginnings. Wear fresh flower wreaths.

Altar Decorations: Vases of flowers, greenery, deity, a basket of dyed red eggs, fresh flower wreaths, small flowering plants in pots. Use green, red, yellow, purple, white, and pastel colors.

Beltane, April 30

> *All is in bud and blossom,*
> *The fairies have wrought their desires,*
> *God and Goddess are wed,*
> *Come dance 'round the Beltane fires.*

Alternate Name: May Eve, High Spring

Primary Themes: (1) The God and Goddess are wed. (2) Celebration of the May Queen. (3) A celebration of the Celtic fire God Belenus. Beginning of the Summer half of the Year.

Agricultural/Historical Themes: Nature has unfurled its green, and flowers bloom. High Spring. Planting continues.

Beltane means "bright fire." The celebration of the Celtic fire God Belenus brings the influences of light and purification. The Welsh God Beli Mawr (Beli the Great) has been identified with Belenus. This was the traditional time to kindle bonfires to encourage growth. In Celtic Britain, livestock were run between bonfires to purify them and keep them sound.

The God Bel may have origins in the consort of the Goddess Astarte. Bael meant Lord. He was originally a sacrificial king. Also, Beltane was a traditional time to mend fences. It is the beginning of the Summer half of the year, when the veil between the worlds is thin. This is the time of fairies, nature sprites, divination, and magic.

Celebration Ideas: The Beltane fire and the Maypole dance are traditional. The Maypole is a great wand, planted in Mother Earth. The Maypole dance was an activity for May Day, the day following Beltane, but I have done it on Beltane in the following way: Atop the pole or three-inch dowel of eight feet in length, attach multicolored ribbons that hang down and touch the ground.

One person sits on the floor and holds the pole. An even number of people take hold of the ribbons and stand away from the pole. Every other person faces the opposite direction. In a sense this creates two groups of people, who are ready to circle the pole in opposite directions. Music starts, either singers or recorded music. The participants begin to circle, going to the left and then to the right of each oncoming person. To the right, left, right, left, weaving the ribbons down the pole, until it is done.

Regarding the Beltane fire, light a fire in an iron cauldron (90 proof alcohol works). You can use a large stainless steel pot. Place a layer of sand at the bottom and then a smaller stainless steel bowl filled with the alcohol inside. Light the alcohol and jump over the flames for a blessing. Or run between two fires and state your blessing. Take care when working with fire. Place tiles or bricks under and around your cauldron.

Altar Decorations: Use any and all spring flowers, greenery, and pots of flowering plants, between which are images of fairies. Use wreaths and ribbons, deity images, symbols of the Sun and Earth in union, gold, and all colors except black.

Summer Solstice, June 21–23

> *Sweet apples and pears*
> *Bend their green leafy branches.*
> *Blooming in perfection are rose and lavender,*
> *Gifts of the Lord and Lady of Summer.*

Alternate Name: Midsummer Festival

Primary Themes: (1) Celebration of the Great Fruitful Mother. (2) The Summer Queen and Summer King together in a perfect union, bearing fruit. Celebration of warm, bountiful Summer days.

Agricultural/Historical Themes: The agricultural field and wild nature are alive with lush beauty and abundance. Animals have been born, and the young feed from their mothers. Fruits and vegetables are gathered in. The grain crops are on their way to maturity.

Summer Solstice celebrates the abundance of the land as well as the heat and light of the Sun, which is at its peak. The God and Goddess are life-giving forces whose union brings us bounty. There was also an early Celtic form of the Sun called Sulis, a Sun Goddess whose name meant "Eye of the Sun."

One Celtic theme for Midsummer was of a battle between the Oak King and the Holly King. At Midsummer the Sun is not only at the height of his power, but he begins to wane; a sacred paradox. The Holly King wins the battle, and when the month of Midsummer is over, the Holly King begins his reign as the year heads toward Winter.

Celebration Ideas: Celebrate one of the themes of Duir the Oak King, such as strength. Light candles to bring the strength of the oak into a particular part of your life. To celebrate Summer's blooming, toss flower petals over participants' heads with a blessing. Give thanks to the Earth Mother and Sun God, and honor the beauty of the Earth.

Honor the Celtic Goddess Badba, who stirs the cauldron of

life. Place the cauldron inside a circle and fill it with the Waters of Life. Have someone become Badba and enchant the waters, adding all good things into it. Then, have Badba ladle some of the water into a small bowl. All should be seated in a circle. In a clockwise direction, each person gives a water blessing. Ask the person to your left what blessing she wants. Then the one with the bowl dips fingers into the water and anoints the forehead of the participant, saying:

> *In the name of Badba,*
> *May good fortune* [or whatever blessing was asked for]
> *Enter your life.*

Pass the bowl and continue around the circle in the same way. Create a symbolic union of Goddess and God as part of your rite by intertwining roses and oak leaves. Say:

> *May the Lord and Lady of Summer,*
> *The Rose and the Oak,*
> *Reign in perfect union!*

Sit in a circle, pass cake or fruit around the circle. Feeding a bit to the one to your left, say:

> *To the fruit of their union!*

Continue all the way around the circle. Create a festive circle dance and end with a feast.

Altar Decorations: Baked bread, bowls of fruit, and lots of fresh flowers such as roses and daisies. Gold and vibrant colors. Images of deity as the Sun, and of a round, fecund Mother Goddess.

Lugnasad: August 1

> *The God (Goddess) of the grain stands tall,*
> *Ripening wheat, and barley all;*
> *The Fertile Mother, crowned in bounty,*
> *The Golden One, in victory*

Alternate Name: Lammas

Primary Themes: Celebration of some early harvest, and of the Earth Mother. Lugh, the many-skilled Celtic Hero-God, was honored.

Agricultural/Historical Themes: Harvest of smaller produce and some early harvest of grain, particularly barley, which ripens earlier than wheat. Nature is beautiful with warm days and great bounty.

This is an early celebration of the grain God, and also of the Celtic Hero-God Lugh (or Lug), the many-skilled and always victorious. In some accounts he was born mortal and was transformed into a God because of his excellence and skill in the arts, in battle, and in moral challenges. In other accounts he was the son of the Celtic Father-God, Dagda. Known as "the shining one," Lugh may have an early connection to Mesopotamian Lugal, a sacrificial King, and a God of death and rebirth.

Lugnasad is also a time of revelry and games, particularly competitive games. This is a good holiday for picnicking and enjoying the warm summer day.

Celebration Ideas: As above, revelry, games, and celebrating out of doors. Fruits and vegetables are ripening and the wheat has grown tall and is on its way to harvest. It is time to honor the God of the Grain, and the victory of a good grain harvest to come. Barley ripens before the wheat, so you can honor the Barley Mother at this time. In late summer, the Earth bears an abundance of foods, so the altar can be filled with baskets of produce.

To celebrate Lugh, try poetic debate of moral questions, ending in divine diplomacy (that's an art!). Entertain each other with riddles. Light candles for good communications or for a victory of justice done.

Try a Spiral Dance. Join hands in a circle (except for the leader and the one at the end of the line). The leader guides the circular line in toward the center, moving in a clockwise spiral. When the center is reached, the leader begins to move in the opposite direction, moving the line into a new spiral, from the center, outward. Sing as you go:

Seed is flowering, grain is ripening,
Lord and Lady to the dance we go!

Altar Decorations: Have bread baked into deity shapes. Fill the altar with the produce of the Earth in baskets and bowls. Have flowers in vases. Use the colors gold, yellow, orange, red, white, green, and/or brown.

Autumn Equinox, September 21–23

Mountain vines whose fragrance bears
A rich sweet scent upon the Autumn air,
And o'er the pleasant vineyards now I gaze,
As for the Earth and all, I give my praise.

Alternate Name: Fall Equinox

Primary Themes: (1) A celebration of the Great Harvest Mother. (2) Giving thanks for her bounty and for the God of the Grain. (3) The sacrifice of the God begins with the harvest sickle.

Agricultural/Historical Themes: Primary grain harvest. Plant life in wild nature has begun its decline. The Goddess is celebrated holding the cornucopia of all good things in this, the primary harvest of the year. The Mother of abundance is the Harvest Queen, such as Greek Demeter and Roman Ceres.

The Lord of the Grain has been reaped, the King is sacrificed. The life-giving reaped grain is tied into bundles and prepared for storage. Pagan sacrificial kings, such as Egyptian Osiris, Sumerian Dumuzi, and Babylonian Tammuz, are all Gods of death and rebirth. They die after the harvest, and annually move through their pattern of death and rebirth, through the power of the Goddess. Her symbol of the sickle becomes the sign not only for harvest but for the death of the God.

Celebration Ideas: On the altar have a large loaf of bread baked as the Goddess. Use nuts, seeds, and dried fruit as decoration. Bring offerings of grains, seeds, dried fruit, and nuts. Give thanks for our gifts, our abilities, and our good fortune. Light candles for prosperity and well-being. Honor the God by saying:

Farewell to the rich yet Waning God.
We honor him for all he gives.
Give thanks for the bounty of the Goddess.
We give thanks to the Harvest Mother,
For her gifts nourish the whole world.
To You who are bounty, beauty, and abundant riches.
To our Mother, the Earth,
To Danu, Ceres, and Demeter, we give thanks.

This is an excellent time to honor the Earth and our interdependency with her. Make agreements to live in ways that are more in harmony with the Earth. Autumn is the time of year to give thanks for what you have. Give thanks for a full cupboard, and for all the blessing that you have reaped.

Create a rite in which you gives thanks for friends, loved ones, teachers, or for all those who serve you in your local or world community. Pass around a cup of wine or juice and toast to them, or pour a libation for each. Name them and create an awareness of how they have given to you and/or to others.

Altar Decorations: Use dried corn, sheaves of grain, autumn leaves, dried gourds, small pumpkins, freshly baked bread in a shallow basket or on a platter, a corn-doll Goddess and a wheat-doll God (or vice versa), a sickle, and the colors red, orange, yellow, brown, gold, and white.

Samhain: October 31

Dark Mother swings her scythe,
The God is dead, and the field is fallow.
Hallowed spirits of the dead,
With food and wine to the Sabbat shall you go!

Alternate Names: All Hallows Eve, Wiccan New Year

Primary Themes: (1) The Goddess as the Dark Mother wields her final scythe. (2) The God journeys to the Land of Death, a Feast of the Dead. (3) The Earth lies fallow in rest and renewal. Beginning of the Winter half of the year.

Earth-Solar Aspects: In the Earth's revolution around the Sun, the northern hemisphere is farther away from the Sun than it was at the previous Sabbat. The nights have lengthened and cooled, and the days have shortened.

Agricultural/Historical Themes: The agricultural field lies barren and wild nature is in decline. This was the time of the last and final harvest, signifying the abundance of the Earth Mother as well as the death of the Grain God. Those animals who appeared too infirm to make it through the Winter were slaughtered and salted. Some of the meat was used at the Samhain feast.

This was the Celtic Feast of the Dead. It was traditional to leave food and wine out for departed ancestors before leaving home for the Sabbat celebration. At this, the beginning of the Winter half of the year, the veil between the worlds is thin. It is a time of ghosts, visitations from the dead, prophecy, divination, and magic.

Celebration Ideas: Have a funeral for the God as he journeys to the Land of Death. Or have someone guide a meditative journey to meet the Dark Mother. Call upon her, seeking knowledge, insight, and wisdom for a specific question or problem. Use the chant:

> *Deep descend, to the Cauldron of Cerridwen.*
> *Deep descend, to Dark Mother's Wisdom.*

Choose a challenge in your life, and do journal writing with deep, honest introspection. If the Moon is waning, use a sickle to "cut away" things you want to release. Or try banishing candle magic with a black candle. Have someone guide a visioning of the Web of Life, and send a group blessing through the Web to someone who needs it, or to a situation that needs it. Or, seated in a circle, use a chant to reach deep trance states. Try the chant *Om-Ma,* or use:

> *Dark Mother Hecate, now enter we*
> *Into Your cavern,*
> *Into Your wisdom.*

Provide a black bowl filled with water and surrounded by candles. Let the chant continue as those who wish to, gaze into the bowl for a vision and give prophesy and blessings. Or divine by using cards, mirrors, or writing prophecy. Light candles for, and give prayers and blessings to departed loved ones, friends, relatives, and pets.

Altar Decorations: Use cauldrons, owls, bats, spiders, black cats, pumpkins, red apples, webs, candles of black, red, orange, yellow, gold, and silver around a black bowl filled with water. Set out foods for the dead.

VII. Magic

This can be magic for a personal need or magic to help others. Use the phase of the moon in this section. If the moon is waning, do a banishing, letting go, or releasing type of magic. If the moon is waxing or full, use a creative, encouraging, building kind of magic. If it is the day of the new moon, or in the first few days of the first quarter, when the new crescent is seen, do magic for blessings or new beginnings.

Doing a visualization of what you seek is a potent form of magic, depending how powerfully you can affirm your vision. There is also candle lighting as a magical act, but there are many resources on the market that teach a variety of magical acts. Here are a few types of candle magic:

Anointing One-Day Candle
Choose your candle colors and scented oils from the appendix on page 197. When anointing a candle with oil, rub the oil onto the bottom half of the candle, then the top half, then around the center, and then the wick.

Write one word on the side of a candle that expresses your wish. Carve it using the point of a knife or any other tool with a sharp point. After you carve your word, take scented oil and rub it into the candle. Do this while stating affirmations for your wish.

Light the candle stating your desire as if it were already completed. Ask for a blessing from your favorite deity.

Three-Day Candle
Light a candle using the oil-anointing process above. Begin the candle on your ritual night. On the first night, state that you are lighting the candle "for" or "so that" a certain goal will be achieved. After several hours, extinguish the candle with a snuffer or small inverted cup, saying:

> *The flame is extinguished but the spell is unbroken.*

Light it the second night and do the same. Light it the third night, strongly visioning the affirmation of your desire. Let the candle burn completely.

Four-Quarter Draw Candle
In the center of your altar place a white candle; this represents you. Place four colored candles evenly around it. Choose the color of the four candles based on your need (see the appendix).

Light the white candle and say:

> *This candle is* [state your name].

Light the other four candles and state your desired goal as follows, for example:

> *Prosperity comes to me from the north,*
> *Prosperity comes to me from the east,*
> *Prosperity comes to me from the south,*
> *Prosperity comes to me from the west.*

Slowly, in four rounds, bring the four candles in toward your center candle. Each time you bring them in, restate the above affirmations for the directions. Bring them in so close that they touch. Follow this with the "Binding Chant" listed under "Chants and Songs" in this chapter. Let the candles burn completely.

Black Candle

Use a black candle for an ending of some kind, to end an unwanted situation. Simply light the candle and say:

> *I light this candle so that _____ may be banished.*

Then say:

> *Power of the Dark Mother attend,*
> *By blade and sickle,*
> *This cord is cut and I am free.*
> *Blessed be.*

Follow this with a bath or shower. Let the candle burn down completely.

Nine-Day Candle

This candle, also called a novena, burns for nine days. This type of candle is widely available. To make it, wax is poured into a tall cylindrical glass and the picture of a deity and prayer are written on it. Mary is a very popular novena. You can buy a white one in plain, clear glass. Paste a prayer and/or a deity picture of your own choosing on it. Place it on your altar, then pray and light your candle. Renew your prayer daily. Let the candle burn down completely.

Drawing-Away Candles

Drawing one candle away from the other can be a form of banishing magic. Choose a white or yellow candle to represent you, and a dark-colored candle for the thing you no longer want in your life. Place the candles next to each other, touching, and in the center of your altar. Light the candles and state the identifications of each. Say:

> *Dark Mother,*
> *Come break the bonds,*
> *And cut away what binds me.*

Then slowly draw them away from each other, repeating the above prayer every so often. Move the candles apart until they are on opposite ends of the altar. Then take a shower or bath. Let the candles burn down completely.

Drawing-Toward Candles
Identify two candles by choosing two separate colors. Use white or yellow to represent you. Choose a second color for what you want to come into your life (this does not include manipulating another person). Place the candles at opposite ends of your altar. Light the candles and state the identification of each. Then say:

> *Great Mother, unite me with my desire.*
> *By your power shall _____ come to me.*

Then slowly draw the candles toward each other. Every so often repeat the prayer. Have the candles come together in the center of your altar. Then state:

> *And so it is.*

VIII. Affirming the Magic

After you perform magic, be it candle magic or a simple visualization, repeat the following nine times, building power as you go.

> *And now by the power of three times three,*
> *As we will it, so shall it be!*

IX. Grounding

To ground the power, you must release energy, thought, and feeling. Completely relax your body into the earth. This needs to be done, or you might find yourself up all night with excess energy.

X. Ceremony of Bread and Wine

This is quite simple—a sharing of bread and wine (or juice), with the traditional sayings. Tear bits of bread off a whole loaf and pass them around and say:

> *May you never hunger.*

Pour wine into cups held by participants and say:

> *May you never thirst.*

You may first want to honor the God and Goddess again, and bless the bread and wine with their love, and in their honor.

XI. Close the Quarters

Begin at the north and go counterclockwise to close each quarter. Face outward of the circle. Hold the wand up with both hands to the quarter. Thank the powers and deities of the direction and let them go.

XII. Open the Circle

The one in the east guides all to say the traditional Wiccan closing:

> *The circle is open, but unbroken!*
> *Merry meet and merry part,*
> *And merry meet again!*

Follow this with a feast.

10

The Crone in
Modern Culture

The women featured in this chapter are examples of wonderful, valuable, elder women. Each has positively affected our society, some through politics, some through their art, others in a wide variety of ways. But they all prove that elder women have "been there," and continue to be there, contributing to our world with their skill, wisdom, and compassion. When possible, we have allowed these remarkable women to tell their stories in their own words.

Beatrice Wood

Potter, Artist, Actress

Beatrice is a fascinating personality. Her independence fueled by her natural curiosity about life and her unique creativity, she defied her Victorian upper-class origins and joined the early twentieth century avant-garde of Paris as an actress. She continued acting in New York and later joined the Greenwich Village art scene. Beatrice made her own way in the world at a time when most women simply married and stayed home. To the end of her days (she lived to be 105) she was creative, strong-willed, compassionate, and filled with the joy of living.

Beatrice was born in 1893 in San Francisco, and died in 1998 in Ojai, California, where she spent the later part of her life. In Ojai, she worked, entertained, and sold her ceramics and drawings. She was always surrounded by friends, students, and many admirers who were intrigued by her talent and coquettish personality.

Beatrice had many influential friends, including the early twentieth-century modern artists Marcel Duchamp and Francis Picabia, as well as French composer and novelist Henri-Pierre Roche. She has been nicknamed "The Mama of Dada," signifying her prominence in the society of Dada artists.

Beatrice began making her famous pottery in the 1930s, but her greatest success with the medium came in her nineties and hundreds. She has been called an alchemist who took clay and created beautiful treasures. Her metallic lusters and methods of firing created glittering rainbow-like golden glazes that light the surfaces of her rustic style of pottery. The contrast of painting sophisticated luster glazes, which is a great art, atop earthy and naive and yet classic forms is a part of her magic. She also created humorous and sometimes lusty figures, as well as drawings.

Beatrice authored two books: *I Shock Myself* (1985), an autobiography, and *Pinching Spaniards* (1988). At the age of 100, she was the photographic subject of a book titled *Playing Chess with the Heart* (1994), in which her witty and wry comments accompanied each photo.

In 1984, Beatrice was declared a "California Treasure." Her work is exhibited in many museums in the United States, including the Metropolitan Museum of Art and the American Craft Museum in New York, the Los Angeles County Museum of Art, the Smithsonian in Washington, D.C., and the Museum of Fine Arts in Boston. Among the international museums that collect and show her work are the Victoria and Albert Museum in London, the Staatliche Museum in Berlin, and The Pompidou Center in Paris.

The Women's International Center honored Beatrice in 1989 with the Living Legacy Award. Her works are also a part of the International Dada Archive. Tom Nell's film *Beatrice Wood: Mama of Dada,* aired on PBS in 1993 and brought Beatrice national acclaim.

The following "wisdoms" are paraphrased from Beatrice's words in *Playing Chess with the Heart:* She wrote that there are three things of utmost importance in life. The first is honesty, which she describes as being able to live without succumbing to the cunning of the mind. The second is compassion. Without compassion, Beatrice says, we have no concern for others and we become monsters. The third is curiosity. Beatrice was a proponent of searching out things, of learning, and in so doing remaining bright and responsive to life.

Sheila Bernard

Mother, Teacher, Political Activist

Sheila Bernard is in many ways an example of a woman warrior, fighting within her own country for what she thinks is right. Her actions test city and state laws and seek to benefit human rights in a sane, just, and logical way. In her personal life, she has learned how to live in the greatest possible harmony with the environment. She exemplifies the qualities of strength, integrity, and justice. Sheila was born in 1949 in Los Angeles. She has three brothers.

My kids are twenty-seven, twenty-four, and eighteen. To their credit, they have grown to be sensitive and caring individuals. I say "to their credit," because I spent many of their childhood years embroiled in the political battle to save the Lincoln Place Apartments where we live. Lincoln Place is a thirty-three-acre, 800-unit, fifty-year-old apartment community housing a diverse population including many seniors and other low-income people. For fifteen years our community has fought off the efforts of the owner to demolish the apartments and replace them with luxury units, which would have displaced two thousand people in the middle of a housing crisis.

I spent much more psychic energy on political issues than I spent raising my kids. In addition I held down a full-time teaching

job for many of those years. In many ways, the kids raised themselves. If I had it to do over again, or if I was to advise other
women, I would tell them to make their kids their first priority.
When you can, as they get older, become involved in the community, but only to the extent that you can bring your children with
you, so they know where you are and who you are, and they feel
that your political life includes them rather than taking your attention away from them.

I have lived a simple, nonmaterialistic, and relatively environ-
mentally benign life. I use organically grown food. I create virtu-
ally no garbage, recycling and composting almost everything, even
to the point of bringing my own cup and cloth napkin to meetings. I changed teaching jobs in order to be able to ride my bicycle
to work. I do what I can to help our society become less auto-
dependent so we can kick the petroleum habit, which is wreaking
havoc in the world.

Petroleum and its derivatives, such as plastics and pesticides,
not only harm our health and the environment; petroleum's ex-
traction from the earth motivates countries to invade and destroy
one another. I believe we are all potential healers of our planet,
and first, we should do no harm. We should avoid like the plague
(and they are a plague) the messages which ooze from the media
saying "Buy! Consume! Spend money on the pretty package!
Then throw it away! You're not good enough! If you don't buy
this product (or treatment or surgery), you will be unworthy of
love! Never mind those tree-huggers! Every Body Needs Milk!
Where's the beef? It's the cheese! You can't eat just one!" I have
done my best to ignore those messages. The planet cannot support the level of consumption that Western cultures enjoy, in addition to the fact that Western corporations parasitically victimize
the Third World in order to support corporate profits and our culture's affluence.

I have become active in the politics of the city of Venice, California, and have been elected to the board of the Grass Roots Venice Neighborhood Council. The neighborhood councils in Los
Angeles advise the City Council on development matters. Therefore,
I have the opportunity to advocate the development of buildings

which help solve our city's housing, water, energy, and transportation problems, and oppose the development of any building which does not contribute to the solution of these problems.

I am also active in Los Angeles politics. I sit on an advisory board for water use, and I attend and provide input to other boards on transportation and recycling, in order to help our city become more harmonious with natural systems.

I have learned to trust my instincts. I have learned that life and everything in it is about love. I have learned to look for the environmental consequences of every social policy. I have learned to trust that my soul lives forever and that everything that happens in this world has more to it than we can perceive.

Raven Ganesha

Teacher, Mother, Sister, Lover, Urban Tantric Shaman

Raven Ganesha is a very generous hearted, compassionate woman with a true gift for seeing with the heart. She has the ability to express thoughts and feelings with Academy Award–worthy passion and power, which allows others to experience their own deep inner well of spirit.

I was born on September 5, 1948, the oldest of three children. Both of my parents independently chose to leave their family's repressive religions, and found identity and comfort in the world of jazz and the 1950's beatniks. They were active in the community, becoming influential in our elementary school, but beyond all else, they valued their family and the love and support that is provided by that unit. I am especially grateful to my mother and my grandmother, who provided an example of truthfulness, strength, and faith that supports me to this day.

I came of age in the 1960s, a time of change and exploration that provided me with a wealth of ideas and possibilities. All that fermentation has fueled my quest for self-process and personal truth. As the Chinese blessing says, I have lived "in interesting times." Growing up in Los Angeles, I now live in Topanga Canyon, an urban wilderness outside of Los Angeles, with my partner, Topanga Pan, and our teenage son, Dylan.

Pan and I conduct monthly shamanic circles for our friends and the general community. We tell the classic myths and stories as a source of enlightenment for our lives. Then, using this as inspiration, we lead a guided journey to discover individual essential truths and spiritual guidance. We often use music and sometimes movement and other artistic expressions to integrate what we learn on these journeys. This has been a challenging pilgrimage in our partnership, allowing us to integrate our spiritual quest with our daily lives, and forcing us to work together very intimately and in deepest respect. The feedback from those who have joined us has been incredibly rewarding.

As a teacher I have touched many children. Since you can't always see the effect you have on children, I always think of it as planting seeds. I may not be around when the seeds that I plant flower and bear fruit, but I have great faith that they will. This is true with all relationships, because as we touch others in whatever way, a seed is planted. I believe my greatest contribution to society is the seeds I have planted and watered liberally with my love. I believe that opening the heart is a constant and awe-inspiring process. The more you let into the heart, the more you can contain.

I also teach Tantric Dance for Women, which has transformed my life and the lives of many other women. Lately Pan and I have realized, largely through our own Tantric work, that Tantric Dance would be extremely valuable for men and women to practice together, as a ritual and as a healing of the patriarchal rift that separates our genders. As valuable as Women's Spiritual Work is for women and Men's Spiritual Work for men, the real challenge is to come together in partnership and mutual respect of our differences, and our similarities. We are going to confront this opportunity and try to develop a curriculum for a class that will benefit both men and women, allowing them to open their hearts and work together to raise their capacity for pleasure, for understanding, and for love.

My Wisdom to share starts in finding your own voice. You might start by discovering other women who have found theirs. In literature read Maya Angelou, Riane Eisler, Marija Gimbutas, Ursula K. Le Guin, Adrienne Rich, Terry MacMillan, Alice Walker, Deena Metzger, Isabel Allende, and Susan Cisneros. Look to women in history who have struggled in a world dominated by men, such as Margaret Mead, Emma Goldman, Eleanor Roosevelt, and Elizabeth Cady Stanton. Look for artists and visionaries that find their own way of negotiating the patriarchy, such as Frieda Kahlo, Tyne Daly, Jane Campion, Georgia O'Keeffe, Riane Eisler, Marija Gimbutas, Margo Anand, and Joan Halifax. Also, talk to your female relatives and find out who the heroines are in your own family. This will feed your search for your own voice.

You might combine this with a study of the Goddess . . . Lady of a Thousand Names. And when you have found her, listen for Her voice, and you will soon know that Her voice is your voice, and that you are She. This work will enable you to liberate your own individual voice that is like no other, and is like all others, because you are Divine and all is one.

Learn a method of relaxation and open lines of communication with your inner truths. You might enjoy Shamanic journeying, creative journaling, self hypnosis, or visualization.

Get to know your body through whatever physical activity draws you. You might pursue Tai Chi, yoga, dance, aerobics, swimming, or other athletics.

Remember that you are Divine. Use this relaxation and physical activity to learn what gives you pleasure, and how to listen to your body. Then trust your body's knowledge. Pleasure is a doorway to the Divine, and you are Divine.

If you are moving into your Cronedom, here are some things that helped me during the transition:

- Examine your relationship to the dark, to death, and to loss. They can become very valuable and comforting. It may be necessary for you to develop new understandings of these natural transitions, or repair old hurts and fears in order to increase your level of compassion for yourself and others. You might want to read Demetra George's book *Mysteries of the Dark Goddess* for guidance and get to know Hecate, Kali, and Demeter.

- Read "When I am an old woman I shall wear purple" by Elizabeth Lucas and "Homage to My Hips" by Lucille Clifton often, perhaps every morning.
- Reinvent yourself. Take up a new endeavor, get a new job, or go back to school. This is the best time to transform yourself. Gail Sheehy's work may be helpful in this.
- Embrace the unfamiliar. This is an ideal time in your life to open up and continue learning new things.
- Look for ways to be in deeper relationship with the earth.
- Continue to remind yourself that all of you is Divine.

Elaine Warford

Mother, Grandmother, Fairy Godmother

Elaine is a kind, polite, intelligent, and wise woman, with a very positive sense of things.

I was born Frances Elaine Howell, July 1951, the youngest daughter of Georgia and Grady Howell. As I grew, despite a deep love of my homeland, I dreamed of the day I could leave Wilson County, Tennessee. Our three-bedroom, one-bath home was situated on the edge of Lebanon, a small town. My two sisters, two brothers, and I all worked on our family's small farm.

We were all brought up with the best of manners and with respect for others. During my later high school years, I enrolled in a school-based Regional Occupation Program (ROP) which provided me the opportunity to work part of the school day and attend school the rest. By that time my parents were divorced, which was quite an accomplishment for my mother, as "proper women" just did not divorce back in those days. Being a proper woman, Mama worked as a nurse's aide in the small mountain community hospital. There, she helped me get a part-time job until graduation when I began making big bucks with full-time employment. The Vietnam War and all of the turmoil of the sixties was wreaking havoc on the world. In 1969 I learned about the music of the sixties, politics in lands far away, and California.

After a short mistake of a marriage, my wonderful daughter

Melissa and I lived with Mama until I found a way to get to California. I was sure it was the only place to raise "Missy" and unheard of opportunities awaited us there. My second husband provided escape. In California, my education then began in earnest. Talk about culture shock! We were working in the upper echelon of the Rock and Roll and very beginnings of the Southern California country rock music business. Years of road trips and raising Missy in recording studios finally got old and my husband eventually became a lawyer as a means of making a living. I worked as a hairdresser, which is how I met my feminist mentor, Vera, who filled me in on all of the women's movement and history-making events that previously passed me by while growing up back home. We worked precincts, marched in the streets, and argued "Are heterosexual women more at odds with other heterosexuals than with lesbians?" or "Why aren't women better friends?" I proudly wore my "Eve was framed" T-shirt and dragged Missy to all the NOW meetings and rallies.

Patricia, my early business mentor, always said, "Money can be your best friend." I realized that I now wanted to go to college, that I needed a degree to finally get ahead. I went to school as I could, finally graduating in 1985. My writing time became sparse and scattered among trying to earn a living, raising Missy, and trying to appease my spouse. Unfortunately, the latter chore robbed me of most of my most productive time; however, I was able to get a few stories published, primarily in magazines.

I got divorced at age forty, and hoped that "my life would really begin." A post-nuptial agreement left me with nothing. I moved back to Tennessee for a few years, to take a job as a Utilization Director of a three-county community mental health center. The "great position" lasted only two years as I was cruelly reminded of all of the reasons that, as an adult woman, I left the South. The women of my generation who were still there had not changed the way they treat one another. So I headed back to California, where I took a job in a small public relations and advertising firm and got into fundraising and politics.

Grandchildren are life's reward for surviving one's youth. My first grandchild was born shortly after my divorce at forty. Kristin Nicole joined us in 1994. Both grandchildren were admitted into their elementary school's "gifted" (whatever that means) program. In so many ways, because of them and my godchildren, I am reassured that there is hope for a kinder future.

These are the wisdoms I would like to share. Always, always, always trust and heed your intuition. I have lived to regret every time that I did not. You cannot love too much. Maybe too little, maybe too long, but not too much. You do not have to love everybody; however, everyone has value, especially if that person is just sorry protoplasm and a lesson in what to avoid. Learn from the mistakes of others. Always wear sunscreen, drink lots of water, and take your vitamins. Try to get a good night's sleep and take a nap when you can. Be generous and cultivate good and true women friends. They will be there when you are old—most men die at a younger age than women. Exercise your mind and body every day. Learn to say no and leave it. Regrets pull you down. Recycle everything you can. Hug whenever possible. Good manners go a long way. With regard to most any negotiation, always leave yourself a "back door." And finally, Say what you mean, mean what you say, but don't say it mean.

Marija Gimbutas

Archaeologist, Teacher, Writer

Scholar and writer Marija Gimbutas was an archaeologist whose work and theories have had an important impact on the history of the evolution of human life and its cultures in the world as we know it today. She did her most significant work in her Crone years, including her on-site excavations in Italy, Greece, and Yugoslavia. A professor of archaeology at the University of California, Los Angeles, she insisted on the highest standards in scholarship, but if anyone could get people passionately interested in the relevance of bones, pottery, and carbon dating, it was Marija. Her graduate seminars always included refreshments and good talk, while at her home in rural Topanga Canyon, she was often hostess to friends, colleagues, and visitors from around the world.

The body of her work encompassed the areas of the Old

Europeans and the Indo-Europeans. The Indo-Europeans were the main forerunners of our present culture and conquered or assimilated the earlier civilization. However, Marija was most interested in the Old Europeans whose culture was formulated around the worship of the Goddess in her various aspects. Her outstanding contribution to the thinking of scholars in her field lay in her ability to connect the physical evidence of archaeology with folklore and mythology, thus gaining insight into how the populations actually thought and acted in their time.

An overall vision of her work is seen in *The Civilization of the Goddess* (1991), in which she states: "My purpose in this book is to bring into our awareness essential aspects of European prehistory that have been unknown or simply not treated on a pan-European scale. This material, when acknowledged, may affect our vision of the past as well as our sense of potential for the present and future. We must refocus our collective memory. The necessity for this has never been greater as we discover that the path of 'progress' is extinguishing the very conditions for life on earth."

Gimbutas was born in Vilnius, Lithuania, in 1921 and earned her Ph.D. in archaeology from Tübingen University in Germany in 1946. She emigrated with her husband to the United States in 1949 though later divorced him. As a researcher at the Harvard University Peabody Museum she published a work on the prehistory of Eastern Europe. Then, offered a teaching position at UCLA in 1963, she crossed the country to Los Angeles with her three daughters, Danuta, Zivile, and Julie. Teaching through the department of Indo-European Studies, she helped develop the Institute of Archaeology and became curator of Old World Archaeology at the UCLA Cultural History Museum.

Author of twenty books and over two hundred articles in the fields of archaeology, Indo-European studies, folklore and mythology, Marija spent her middle and later years firmly grounded in her work of archaeological excavation, which she made at Obre, Bosnia,1967–68; Anza and Sitagroi in Macedonia, 1968–70; Achilleion in Thessaly, Greece, 1973–74; and Scaloria in Southeastern Italy, 1978–80.

She developed several important theories with regard to beliefs, migration of peoples, and languages in the areas that she studied.

In her works on the Eastern European, Aegean, and Mediterranean areas of Mesolithic, Neolithic, and Copper Age cultures, she increasingly found the "pre-eminent role of a Mother-Goddess cult." This analysis developed into her 1989 volume on folk symbolism, myth, and religion entitled *The Language of the Goddess.*

In the field of Indo-European studies, one of her outstanding contributions is known as the "Homeland" theory, which posits that the Indo-Europeans migrated out of the area of the Russian Steppes in several waves beginning around 4500 B.C. These patri-archal, warlike groups were notable for the *kurgans*, or mound burials, found along their route, which were different from the burial sites of the original population. Gimbutas was concerned with a very different culture pervading Europe and environs in the Paleolithic and Neolithic eras, which spoke through its remaining artifacts. The culture was based in a Neolithic Goddess-centered religion, having roots in an earlier age. This religion, different from the ones that came subsequently, is harmonious with nature. It was practised by a society with a basically egalitarian social structure that coexisted peacefully with its neighbors. The advent of the Indo-Europeans brought with it much thinking that remains to the present day. Their religion was male centered and their social structure had hierarchies of power, from lowest to highest.

Gimbutas's last major publication before her death in 1994 was the lavishly illustrated *The Civilization of the Goddess: The World of Old Europe*, which focuses on Neolithic European cultures organized into geographic and cultural areas. As a synthesis of excavation materials, it includes much helpful data, including a listing of over 200 cultures and major sites from Lepenski Vir to Stonehenge.

Marija had many friends and colleagues who enjoyed working with her. Miriam Dexter, who edited and supplemented Marija's book *The Living Goddesses* (published posthumously), said that one of the most remarkable things about her was her energy. She researched exhaustively, and she was always reading a manuscript for someone. She had a seminar for students who were preparing papers for the international conferences she organized in Europe. Marija was very generous. She gave great parties.

A colleague who was with her on several digs said she was a very enthusiastic archaeologist and terrific in the field. She put up cheerfully with difficult and uncomfortable environmental conditions. Marija was interested in many countries and managed to travel all over the world. She had visited all the countries in Eastern Europe and knew a great many languages (living and dead), which facilitated her travels. She was always enthusiastic about her projects and very involved in whatever she did.

Pat Russell

Filmmaker, Mother, Counselor

Pat Russell lives in a blue house on Malibu Lake in Agoura, California, with three dogs and a friendly wild goose called Bouba. She was born in Akron, Ohio, on June 10, 1943. She graduated from the University of Wisconsin with a degree in social work, psychology and drama. Pat became interested in acting when she went to sign up for an art class and instead walked into the Dramatic Arts department, where one of the teachers persuaded her to take an acting class. "When I went to Boston to work as a social worker for the Massachusetts Commission for the Blind, I took acting classes at night and would do scene study." After she got married, she moved to New Jersey. "It was only a hop, skip, and a jump to New York City, so I started taking acting classes with Herbert Berghoff. In the beginning my husband didn't like it and would put me down for it. Luckily, there was another lady in his life that took him away from me. Now I look back and think she was an angel that got him out of my life . . . because I probably would not have had the guts to get him out as quickly."

Pat moved to New York and got an apartment on Jane Street in the Village with some friends. She took classes and auditioned for parts. "But I was getting tired of the kind of parts available for women, which were mostly really degrading. Plus, I was getting tired of casting directors and agents coming on to me over and over again. It . . . hurt you almost like psychic rape." She decided to take a class in film production, but it turned out to be more of an ego trip for the instructor, and a way to get a free crew, so she applied to N.Y.U. Graduate Film School. One of seven women and twenty-eight men chosen for the class, she said, "I knew it was going to be a struggle, because the men had an attitude that women couldn't possibly be good filmmakers. So we had to fight much harder in order to get our crews together and to get the equipment, and it made us tougher and better.

"When it was time to screen the films, the women's films were so far superior to the guys', because they were from their heart and not from wanting to be another Spielberg. In fact, when my film was being screened, this guy said, 'How come her film is so good? My film isn't that good. She's a girl. She's a woman. How come?'

"My first little film was called *Just Married*, and was a spoof on the American wedding reception. As soon as the couple is married, the whole dynamic changes between them and the power trips begin. They end up having a cake fight, pulling off their clothes and running into the woods. It won a Cine Golden Eagle and went on to represent the United States in a bunch of film festivals. It won in Germany and Scotland, so it was a really good thing to have happen."

For her second film, *Sally at 13*, she decided to work on something about her teenage life, "because it was such a tumultuous period of identity. It's the story of a thirteen-year-old girl growing up in the fifties, and it had all those issues that teens have to deal with. When this one girl, Irene Arranga, walked in, she blew my mind, she was so good, and I knew that I had a good movie, because I had the right lead to play Sally." The rest of the cast was around twelve or thirteen, but Pat found after the audition that Arranga was really twenty-one. "It didn't matter, because she was so good. She burned a hole in the screen." When the cinematography teacher, Beta Batka, asked her what she was going to do for her second semester, she replied, "I shot the film the first semester and I'm going to edit it the second semester. He said, 'No, no, no, no. You should do another movie. You should go shoot. Shoot, shoot!' I said, 'Shoot what?' He said, 'Go write another script. You've got all this talent and all these students and you've got all this equipment.' So that's when I started the feature film."

Pat started writing a script and decided that she was the only person she could count on to be there every day in almost every scene for no money, so she cast herself in the lead. "It's really basically autobiographical . . . I thought if I'm going to do this movie, it's about honesty, and I have to not be ashamed of anything happening to me growing up . . . so I made a commitment to make the story totally honest, but I didn't make it exactly like my own story. You have to change it to make a screenplay, but it was very close, like the bad marriage to a control freak and my parents both being alcoholics. Basically, I wanted to tell how you can grow up in insanity, and then you can escape into other insanity, which was the marriage, and then finally hit bottom, so that you have to become your own person or you die. That was the story, because I know that if I hadn't gotten in touch with my creative nature, I would have died.

"*Reaching Out* was a work of love, and everybody that worked on it loved working on it because they knew that we were making a film that had something to say. A lot of these people worked on horror films and exploitation films and hated them. I didn't have time to worry about the acting. I was in the character instantly . . . It was actually me, maybe fifteen years before. . . . When the film was finished we had a screening, and it was such a wonderful experience. It felt really affirming, sort of like how you feel when you're out in the rain and it's really warm. You can tell if people like it, because that's why you become a filmmaker. Because you want to connect with the audience and have some kind of emotional effect on them.

"Then I started screening it for distributors, but I didn't do it very well. I didn't know what I know now about how to position films, and I didn't have a producer's rep. I was told that a film that didn't have any sex, action, violence, or stars would have a hard time. A couple who were distributors considered it, and the woman said, 'I loved your movie. I totally related to it, but my husband hated it, because it reminded him of himself, and he can veto what we distribute.' Many critics really were favorable to it. Roger Ebert saw it at the Sundance Film Festival and gave it a great quote in 1982."

Pat attended the Sundance festival its first year, in 1978, when it was called the United States Film Festival. (It became the

Sundance Film Festival seven years later when Robert Redford took it over.) Pat said that director "John Cassavetes had already told me that someone had to develop a great film festival to really honor independent film. He knew that, too, because he was a pioneer." That was the year Pat met Eagle, who later became the father of her son John. "Eagle's film *The Whole Shootin' Match* tied for first place with Claudia Weil's *Girlfriends*.

Pat was also a founding member of the Independent Film Project (IFP), in 1979. She says, "I got in touch with Sandra Schulberg, who was putting it together. We spent two weeks brainstorming about how we would have this independent feature project. I kept telling them distribution was the most important thing, because I had already found out how difficult it was, and we talked about how we needed alternative distribution for independent films." They decided on showing films at a film market. Sandra was too busy working on a film at the time, so Pat put it together. "I programmed eighteen films and put them on at Magno Screening Room right at the same time as the New York Film Festival. The buyers would come from the New York Film Festival to our little market and say, 'Hey, these films are much more interesting.' It was a huge success that year and has become the biggest screening of independent films besides Sundance."

Pat showed *Reaching Out* at the Cannes Film Festival the next year. Then, New Yorker Films decided to distribute it. But the story didn't end there. New Yorker pulled out of the distribution contract when they thought they couldn't sell it. Then the theater she paid to screen it threw her out when the film got panned by the *New York Times*.

Pat kept on believing in the film and having screenings. She got an offer from another distributor, but it was not a good deal, so she didn't take it. She says not getting distribution "makes me look like a loser, but I'm not a loser. I was a warrior."

Her son John was born on June 10, 1979, on her birthday, which makes them both Geminis. She says, "We have double twins in the family. It's a challenge, because of all that Gemini energy, and we've had to learn to deal with it and not be threatened by it." Pat moved to Los Angeles when her son turned six. She produced and directed cable TV shows for Women in Film and wrote about the Sundance Festival for the organization's monthly news magazine, *Reel News*. During this time, she worked with the Coalition for the Prevention of Violence, a Los Angeles County organization. "I was head of their media division, and I put on conferences and got panels with famous people to talk about how violence in the media affects children. We were in touch with government officials. I think it's helped, because they've done all these studies now and they think it's true, and there's all this legislation about trying to help protect children."

The film *Sally at 13* got distributed all around the country to museums, schools, and libraries, but Pat says the lack of distribution for her feature made her actually want to quit the business for a while. She got another Masters degree in Marriage, Family and Child Counseling, because "I was just so fed up with the shallowness of the movie business and such little reward for so much effort. I became an intern therapist and worked at Tarzana Treatment Center counseling addicts. This was when my son was eight years old, before I ever dreamt I'd have to be dealing with his addiction, and in a way it prepared me to be a better mother and a more enlightened person, dealing with addiction in my own family. My parents were addicts. I'm an addict, but I'm addicted to film, instead."

Pat is now shooting a documentary called *Transcendence,* about her son's addiction to alcohol and "his struggle to get free of it and transcend it through self-understanding and through facing consequences. It's really his journey. He's very verbal . . . My son wants to be an actor and eventually a writer/director. I'm surprised. I encouraged him to pursue his talent, but I never pushed him. He was in a play when he was younger, and an agent discovered him and set him up to get commercials, but he wasn't happy about it and didn't like to go to auditions, so I said it was fine if he didn't go."

Pat's words of wisdom are: "I think one of the most important things I learned is to have patience and tenacity and at the same time not put your personal self-worth on what happens in your career. It's an outside force that you can't control. Separate who you really are from whether or not you are 'successful' in the business you pursue, because who you are is something much deeper than anything you're doing. I think it's hard to remember that some-times because we all get caught up in that part of our ego selves. Recognition and success are part of a game we play in the world and it's good to say 'I've played the game as well as I could.' "

Henriette Worsfold

Librarian, Mother, Mountain Climber

Henriette Worsfold was born in a little city in Holland called Bredya on January 20, 1918, the third child in the family. Her parents were Catholic, so she attended a Catholic school. Some of the teachers were nuns and some were lay teachers. "We had our own building, and next to us was the school for the poor." She didn't approve that it was separate. "They had a strange custom. On Christmas one of the students was dressed by us. We bought the clothes for him. I found it kind of humiliating for the child who was picked.

"After elementary school, I went to boarding school . . . a gymnasium, which is a secondary school that prepares students for college. It was a good school. We wore uniforms, black on Sunday and navy blue on weekdays. We had Greek, Latin, French, English, and Dutch, and we also had PE (physical education), so I liked school. After graduation, I wanted to go to college, but by that time, we were invaded. We had German occupation. World War II had started, and eventually the Germans closed the universities and sent the students to Germany to work."

Henrietta wanted to become a college teacher, but she finally decided to become a librarian. The library school was not connected to the university, so it was still open. She attended four years, "three to become an assistant and one more if you wanted to be a head librarian. It was not what I really wanted, but I liked people and I liked books, so I had a good time." She spent her final year at the Hague and worked in the Royal Library and others there.

"After the war, I was very anxious to get away from Europe, so I applied for a job in the West Indies. It was a part of the Dutch

Kingdom. I did go, and it was a very happy part of my life, because I was popular and we danced a lot. It was [something] I didn't have when I was younger." She wanted to stay no longer than six years, so she went back to Holland, spending a few years in Amsterdam.

In the meantime, her sister had gone to the United States. "I was beginning to be restless again. I wanted to go to the United States, and she was in Los Angeles. I thought it would be nice to go there. My sister was working for U.S.C. (University of Southern California). She talked about me to them, and I got a job at U.S.C. as a librarian.

"It was lovely to be on the campus, and again I had a great time, but they paid so very little. I thought I couldn't even have a decent apartment with the amount that I made. I decided to move on, and it was actually for the money. So I did go and work for the Braille Institute. It was also an interesting experience, but I preferred the university.

"My favorite thing to do is reading, and I'm taking classes at the Culver City Senior Center in French and German, just to brush up on them. I also take Tai Chi. I was a mountain climber. [I] climbed here . . . with the Sierra Club. Two years ago, I had to quit. I was eighty-two then. I did it with two old timers. One was seventy-nine, but he was very strong. He helped, so I never even stumbled, but this was in the Santa Monica mountains. They're easier. We used to go to the Angeles Crest Forest and climb mountains every week."

Ida Miller

Dancer, Teacher, Great-Grandmother

"I was named Ida after my Dad's ex girlfriend. She was a burlesque dancer. My Mom used to tease me about that. She told me, 'That's why you can dance so good.' " Ida Miller was born on July 10, 1924, in Auburn, New York, where her father owned a trucking company. In 1939, the family moved to Los Angeles. Ida had pains in her legs every winter. At that time they called it rheumatism. "They said it never rains in Los Angeles. It's always sunshine, and maybe it will help your rheumatism. That's why we moved down here."

Ida went to Santa Monica High School through ninth grade. She was fifteen and her husband was eighteen when she got married. "We were married fifty-six years, and he was a wonderful guy." Her mother didn't want her to get married, because she said she was just a baby, "but when they saw how good he was to me, they were just crazy about my husband. He worked for the City of Santa Monica as an assistant supervisor at Woodlawn Cemetery on Pico Boulevard. He was in charge, and sometimes it was depressing. It took five or six months of testing to get the job, and out of five hundred, they picked three." The couple lived in Santa Monica and moved to their house in Culver City in 1950. Ida has four children—three boys and a girl—and two great-grandchildren.

When she first came to California, Ida joined a tap-dancing group called the Meglin Kiddies. They had a tap-dancing studio, and the lessons were twenty-five cents an hour. "During the war my girlfriend and I danced at the canteens and at the Marine base at Port Hueneme.

"My friend opened up a studio . . . She was teaching me a routine, and when I was done I just passed out . . . I was pregnant with my last baby. I've been working since I was fifteen years old. I'd have my children and go right back to work . . . I was seventeen when I had my first child." Ida worked at The Dome in Ocean Park, an amusement pier in Santa Monica. She was an usher in a movie theater there and at the Rosemary Theater in Venice. "I liked the Dome, because they had the Aragon Ballroom, and I used to go there and jitterbug. They had Artie Shaw, Benny Goodman, and all the bands.

"After the second baby, I went to work in a machine shop, and then I was a camera girl at the Moulin Rouge night club. It's in Hollywood. Then I tap-danced at Ben Blue's night club on Wilshire. My husband wasn't a dancer, and people couldn't figure out why I married someone who wasn't a dancer. Well, I loved him. That's why."

Besides her regular job, she worked weekends for a caterer at temples like Beth Israel on Wilshire and one at the Farmer's Market. She had her last job for fifteen years as a manager at a company that printed post cards. She was in charge of the shipping department and retired at the age of sixty-two.

One day she went to the Culver City Senior Center and they asked her to teach there. "I was in the office and Adelle said to me, 'Ida, do you know how to tap-dance?' " When she said that she could, she was asked to take over the class, because the teacher was on vacation for a month. She didn't remember many of the steps she had done, so she made up a dance of the wooden soldiers and taught it to the class. Later, the regular teacher became ill, so Ida was asked to teach the class permanently. That was in 1989, and she's still teaching it. "We are the Culver City Tap Dancing Seniorettes. We go to convalescent homes and perform at the Center.

"You don't have to do exercises for tap," she explains. "You just get right into it, but you have to have tap shoes. I make up all the steps and all of the dances . . . Adelle and I used to do tap routines. We have eleven dancers in the Seniorettes . . . Making up the dances takes a lot of time."

Ida teaches classes every Tuesday and works at Meals on Wheels on Mondays and Fridays. "We take meals to people who can't go out shopping for themselves. One gal drives, and I do the delivery. I love it. I told my kids, 'I don't get a penny for this, but it's the best job I ever had in my whole life, and the people are so nice.' "

Another project of Ida's was assistant tour guide for A.A.R.P., which goes on day trips around the city. She also sailed on one of their cruises to the Panama Canal. When she went to the Breakfast Club in Los Angeles, a man from the Club came up to her and said, "You look like a tap dancer." "There were about five hundred people there," says Ida, "so I got up on the stage with him, and we did *Tea for Two*."

Ida's life became more difficult in the last few years. "I lost my husband and then my mom, my brother, then my daughter-in-law, my cousin, and my niece, all in two years." Ida had breast cancer, and her husband got cancer, too. "I thought I was the first one to go, but I got well and he didn't." Her children helped her. "I've been lucky to have them . . . It was terrible. That's why every once in a while I don't feel so good." She is still tap-dancing, though.

For her words of wisdom, she says, "When you are young, everything takes on more importance. When you're not as young as you used to be, it's not that serious. You may have problems, even someone dying, but you should just go on with your life. I tell my students, 'Just keep on tap-dancing!' When things don't work out, think about all the good things, don't think about the bad things . . . Think, I want to remember this step or that step. I want to be a good tap dancer. I'll say to them, 'All right, you did really badly. Go into the office. I'm going to tell the principal.' And they start cracking up laughing . . . I'm only joking; we have a lot of fun."

Epilogue

In this book we have ventured into territory that has not been given enough attention in our culture: the time of the Crone in the life of women. It is indeed a time of self- examination, because understanding is important in order to go forward with a sense of self-love and determination.

We have discussed the importance of looking within and examining our lives, our strengths and weaknesses, our hopes and fears, our regrets and our desires for the future. Doing this frees us to bypass any patterns that have not been beneficial to us and to take a step (or a leap) forward into what we really want in life. We have examined the history of attitudes toward the Crone and gotten acquainted with women who have evolved in their Cronehood. We have faced physical mortality and embraced our spiritual immortality. Crone Goddesses, icons of a variety of cultures and peoples, have offered us their wisdom and magic.

We have deepened our Cronehood through the creative magic of useful crafts and enlarged our vision through ritual and meditation. Now is the time to envision our future beyond the limitations our culture may have placed on us. Bypassing old stereotypes frees us to be true to our own visions. Is there some dream we have left unrealized that we can now work on? What about that great project we always wanted to accomplish but were afraid couldn't be done? Perhaps it can be created now. In the process of accomplishment, we may gain what we were looking for all along. In addition, we have learned to deal with life's difficulties as gracefully as we can.

What about those pleasures we never really gave ourselves? This is a good time to see them come to fruition. It is also a time to think of ourselves, relax, step back, and take a look around us. As Crones we may find that some of the pressures of life are removed, or we may need to make changes in our lives to remove some of those pressures. This gives us the ability to focus on future visions.

As each season comes and goes, it can be celebrated, for it is a part of the ebb and flow of our lives and the lives of all on Earth. So as we celebrate the ongoing seasons, we can imagine and embody our visions in a new way that is unique to this time of life. We understand the seasons that have gone before, and we can use our sense of magic to shape the life of our future. Hail to the Magical Crone!

Appendix: Fragrances and Candle Colors

I. Fragrant Oils and Incense

COURAGE AND SUCCESS: Heliotrope, rosemary, High John

HEALING AND VITALITY: Rosemary, carnation, pine, sandalwood

MONEY AND PROSPERITY: Patchouli, mint, bergamot, almond, High John

PEACE: Gardenia, rose, hyacinth, lilac

LOVE: Rose, jasmine, sweetpea, lavender, violet

EROTIC LOVE: Musk, patchouli, vanilla

PURIFICATION: Cedar, frankincense, myrrh, cinnamon, rosemary, sandalwood

SPIRITUALITY: Sandalwood, frankincense, myrrh, violet, gardenia

PROTECTION: Wisteria, anise, sandalwood, cinnamon, cloves, cedar

FERTILITY: Patchouli, musk, strawberry, orange

BANISHING: Frankincense, rosemary, cloves, dragonsblood palm

HAPPINESS: Cyclamen, sweetepea, hyacinth

II. Colors for Candles and Ritual Themes

WHITE: Purity, new beginnings, peace, truth, birth, rebirth, sincerity

BLACK: Letting go, endings, banishings

RED: Love, lust, birth, vitality, creativity, power, strength, passion, life

PINK: Love, friendship, goodwill

ORANGE: Confidence, magnetism, power, joy, attracting, inspiration

YELLOW: Confidence, success, centered power, happiness

GREEN: Health, wealth, riches, fertility, well-being, joy

LIGHT BLUE: Peace, gentle communications, patience, understanding

BLUE: Good communications, speaking truth, wisdom

VIOLET/PURPLE: Psychic powers, spirituality, divination, wisdom

BROWN: Grounding, balance, calm

Bibliography

Baring, Ann, and Jules Cashford. *The Myth of the Goddess.* New York: Viking Arkana, Penguin Books, 1991.

Branston, Brian. *Gods of the North.* New York: Vanguard, 1955.

Conway, D. J. *Maiden, Mother, Crone.* St. Paul, Minn.: Llewellyn, 1994.

Cunningham, Scott. *Cunningham's Encyclopedia of Magical Herbs.* St. Paul, Minn.: Llewellyn, 1990.

————. *The Complete Book of Incense Oils and Brews.* St. Paul, Minn.: Llewellyn, 2000.

de Gruyter, Walter. *Origins of the Greek Religion.* Berlin, New York: Walter de Gruyter, 1973.

Edgerton, Franklin. *The Beginnings of Indian Philosophy.* Cambridge, Mass.: Harvard University Press, 1970.

Ferguson, John C. "Chinese Mythology," in *Mythology of All the Races.* Boston: Archaeological Institute of America, Marshal Jones, 1928.

Fettner, Ann Tucker. *Potpourri, Incense and Other Fragrant Concoctions.* New York: Workman, 1977.

Fontana, David. *The Secret Language of Symbols.* San Francisco: Chronicle, 1993.

Gimbutas, Marija. *The Language of the Goddess.* San Francisco: Harper & Row, 1989.

———— with Miriam Robbins Dexter. *The Living Goddesses.* Los Angeles: University of California Press, 1999.

————. *The Civilization of the Goddess.* New York: HarperCollins, 1991.

Graves, Robert. *The Greek Myths.* New York: George Braziller, 1957.

Gwin & Jones, trans. *The Mabinogion.* New York: Alfred A. Knopf, 2000.

Hogan, Elizabeth L., & Joseph F. Williamson, eds. *Sunset Western Garden Book.* Menlo Park, Calif.: Sunset, 1994.

Hollier-Larousse. *World Mythology.* Paris: Library Larousse, 1965.

Katlyn. *The Scented Altar.* Las Vegas: Mermaid Magical Arts, 1993.

Kerenyi, Karl. *Athene. Virgin and Mother in Greek Religion.* Dallas: Spring, 1978.

Kinsley, David. *Tantric Visions of the Divine Feminine.* Berkeley: University of California Press, 1997.

Larrington, Carolyne, ed. *The Feminist Companion to Mythology.* London: Pandora, HarperCollins, 1992.

Luck, George. *Arcana Mundi.* Baltimore: Johns Hopkins University Press, 1985.

Mason, Adrienne. *The World of the Spider.* San Francisco: Sierra Club Books, 1999.

Oldfield, Howey M. *The Cat in the Mysteries of Religion and Magic.* New York: Castle, 1956.

O'Toole, Christopher, ed. *The Encyclopedia of Insects.* New York: Facts on File, 1986.

Reif, Jennifer. *Song to Tara,* "Mysteries of Earth (a.c.)." Los Angeles: Memosyne Recording, 1992.

Sadler, William A. *The Third Age.* Cambridge, Mass.: Perseus, 2000.

Sheehy, Gail. *New Passages.* New York: Random House, 1995.

Stepanich, Kisma K. *Fairy Wicca,* Books I & II. St. Paul, Minn.: Llewellyn, 1994 & 1995.

Stutley, Margaret. *Harper's Dictionary of Hinduism.* New York: Harper & Row, 1977.

McDaniel, June. *The Madness of the Saints; Ecstatic Religion in Bengal.* Chicago & London: University of Chicago Press, 1989.

McTaggart, Lynne. *What Doctors Don't Tell You.* New York: Avon Books; HarperCollins, 1998.

Metzner, Ralph. *The Well of Remembrance.* Boston: Shambhala, Inc., 1994.

Meyer, W. Marvin, ed. *The Ancient Mysteries; A Sourcebook.* San Francisco: Harper & Row, 1987.

Turcan, Robert. *The Gods of Ancient Rome.* Edinburgh: Edinburgh University Press, 2000.

United States Census Bureau. *Statistical Abstract of the U.S.* Washington, D.C.: Department of Commerce, 2000.

Vijay, Fadia, ed. *Healthy Immune System.* Torrance, Calif.: Homestead Schools, 2002.

Walker, Barbara. *The Crone.* New York: Harper & Row, 1985.

———. *The Women's Encyclopedia of Myths and Secrets.* San Francisco: Harper & Row, 1983.

Welk, Stephen R. *Medusa: Solving the Mystery of the Gorgon.* New York: Oxford University Press, 2000.

Index